JAMMING WITH CULTURE

MEDIUM

Rare

KEN ROCKBURN

Stoddart

Published in 1995 by
Stoddart Publishing Co. Limited
34 Lesmill Road
Toronto, Canada
M3B 2T6
Tel. (416) 445-3333
Fax (416) 445-5967

Stoddart Books are available for bulk purchase for sales promotions,
premiums, fundraising, and seminars. For details, contact the
Special Sales Department at the above address.

Canadian Cataloguing in Publication Data

Rockburn, Ken
Medium rare

ISBN 0-7737-5752-X

1. Medium rare (Radio program). 2. Celebrities –
Canada – Anecdotes. 3. Celebrities – Canada –
Interviews. 4. Popular culture – Canada – Anecdotes.
I. Title.

PN1991.77.M43R6 1995   791.44'72   C95-931159-9

Cover Design: Bill Douglas/The Bang
Computer Graphics: Tannice Goddard/S.O. Networking
Printed and bound in Canada

"I Wonder How Many People in This City" and "Days of Kindness"
from *Stranger Music* by Leonard Cohen. Used by permission
of the Canadian Publishers, McClelland & Stewart.

*Stoddart Publishing gratefully acknowledges the support of the
Canada Council, the Ontario Ministry of Culture, Tourism,
and Recreation, Ontario Arts Council, and Ontario Publishing Centre
in the development of writing and publishing in Canada.*

For Sheila,
Lauren, and Ellis —
my public

Contents

Acknowledgements

"Medium Rare" was first a radio show, then a book. Many people were responsible for easing the way for both: Chuck Azzarrello and Steve Colwill at CHEZ FM, who let me start producing "Medium Rare"; Harvey Glatt, who owns the joint; Brian "The Source" Murphy, who gave up two hours of his territory; John Metcalf, who was the first one to think of it as a book; Paul King, who knows the size of the real universe; Powell Kirby, Bubba (The Hyperbolator), and Brownstein, the left-coast support group; the appropriately named Angel Guerra; and Lynne "Queen of the Comma" Missen.

I would like to thank the Ontario Arts Council for its assistance.

Portions of "The Lion in Winter" appeared in *Quarry* magazine, Volume 42: Number 3.

The profile of Daniel Lanois first appeared in *Metro* magazine.

Introduction:
A Centrifugal
Bumblepuppy

At one o'clock in the afternoon on October 9, 1990, I interviewed Timothy Findley about his book *Inside Memory*. It was a Tuesday, overcast, a bit on the cool side.

No, this isn't an endorsement of one of those super memory gimmicks you see on late-night TV infomercials with a fading talk show host looking perpetually amazed. I can recall the details of this particular interview because my son, Ellis, had entered the world two hours earlier at the Ottawa Civic Hospital. I had been with my wife all night and when I made it to the radio station for the Findley interview, I was exhausted, elated, strung-out, and distracted, but I was damned if I was going to miss a chance to talk to a writer I had long admired. After I explained my state, Findley reached for my copy of his book and dedicated it to my new son on the day of his birth. Three years later, when I next spoke with Timothy Findley, he graciously said he recalled the event. It is doubtful that he actually did, but he is a man of much class.

Findley is just one of many, many authors I have been lucky enough to have interviewed in my career — not to mention songwriters, actors, and some just plain famous people. With the exception of one brief year when my radio program, "Medium

Rare," was carried by radio stations in five other cities, these interviews were heard only in Ottawa on CHEZ FM, where I was news director for more than a decade.

It is almost too easy for me to be submerged in the flood of memories flowing from those years.

I remember calling writer Brian Doyle to ask if he would come in and record a poem about baseball by the late American poet Richard Hugo. It was a very evocative poem about a bunch of middle-aged men playing softball in the dimming light of a summer evening. Doyle's voice, I thought, would be ideal. He arrived wearing his trademark windbreaker and cloth cap and asked me if he could read it through a few times before we taped. For the next half hour, staff at the radio station were startled and amused to see this big bear of a man, cap and jacket still on, reading glasses perched on the end of his nose, wandering the halls reading this poem aloud. His rendition, when finally taped, was near perfect. I still bring the tape out and listen to it every so often.

I remember the studio door slowly opening seconds before I was to go live on-air with the Godfather of Soul, James Brown, and being beckoned over by the music director who hissed at me, "*Don't* call him James. He likes to be called *Mr. Brown*!"

I was wearing the only set of headphones in the studio. As the interview began, Brown — sorry, *Mr. Brown* — kept demanding, "Are we on? Are you sure we're on?"

"Sure," I replied, holding my headphones towards him so he could hear himself. Then, trying to lighten it up, I said, "Man, are you sure you really own a bunch of radio stations?" The Hardest Working Man in Show Business fixed me with the meanest glare I have ever seen. Lucky for me he wasn't packing a piece.

I remember finishing a particularly good interview with Dr. David Suzuki and he said, "That was great! You must be American!"

And I remember, back before "Medium Rare" began, dragging George Jonas, magnificent and oh-so-European in his squeaky leather motorcycle jacket, down to the newsroom on October 19, 1981, to stand amidst the entire radio station staff to watch Rick Monday belt his one-run homer to give the Los Angeles Dodgers the win and rob the Expos of the National League East pennant. Jonas, not a baseball fan, kept whispering, "What's going on? What are they doing?" Not what you would call a baseball fan either, I could only smile cryptically.

I've always liked books and I've always been endlessly fascinated with the writing process. I had the good fortune in my teens to be surrounded by guys who appreciated a good line of prose or a good song lyric. Through much of my poverty-stricken twenties I frequented secondhand bookstores; in my thirties, as an interviewer, I felt blessed to be getting free books and the opportunity to talk to the writers of those books. I once hired a sports reporter because he was easily fifteen years younger than me, yet he recognized the poster on my office wall as Jack Kerouac. How could I not hire him?

This appreciation of writing, this respect for the effort and discipline needed to create a written work, exacted its own demands on me. I realized early on that the tours authors must make to promote a new book are far too often characterized by breezy interviews and ill-read interviewers just going through the motions to fill six or eight minutes of air time. Imagine spending months, maybe years, sitting alone in a room in front of a blank piece of paper, conjuring up new and wonderful stories and plots and juxtapositions of words and phrases, only to be confronted time and again by interviewers who had not bothered to read the words you had agonized over.

This will not be my style, I swore. *I will read everything*, I pledged. And to a large extent I kept those promises.

But. There is always a *but*.

Before I give the impression that I was the insufferable martyr to the twice-yearly avalanche of books unloaded onto the media, let me relate a sobering and — certainly for me — chilling story of an interview that was nearly catastrophic. It will put what follows in the rest of this book into perspective.

It was a warm summer day in June of 1989 and the newsroom was abnormally busy for that time of year. Parliament was still sitting, various local stories were developing, and our six-person newsroom was functioning with one less body. This small staff was responsible for covering Parliament, City Hall, and other regional governments, writing and reading regular lengthy newscasts throughout the day, and arranging and recording interviews for a daily hour-long public affairs program that I hosted at six o'clock each evening. This was on top of my own preparations for "Medium Rare." It was often a busy place, and the absence of just one staffer made it more so.

Checking my appointment book early in the day, I saw a notation reading "Green Book." A quick scan of my bookshelf revealed a book on recycling written by an ex-Pollution Prober. An easy interview. So easy, in fact, that I decided I should be doing more pressing things and convinced the host of the station's entertainment and lifestyles program that this could just as easily be one for her show, rather than mine. Having disposed of the interview, I put it out of my mind.

A few hours later, as I was busily editing tape in the newsroom, my colleague strolled in looking entirely too smug.

"I don't think this is the interview you thought it was," she smiled. "I think you can have it back."

"What do you mean?"

"I took this very nice man into the studio and started asking him about composting and he looked confused, then he smiled and said, 'I think you have the wrong person, my dear.'"

"So who is he?" I could feel the panic starting to rise.

"His name is Norman Sherry and he's written a biography of Graham Greene."

Good God. The *Greene* Book. Not the Green Book. I bolted from the room to my office. There it was on an upper shelf. It was very big. Not counting the appendix, it was 725 pages. The cover said, "Volume One." I was sunk. This was a book that looked like it would take two people to lift and I hadn't even cracked its spine. My chest was feeling remarkably tight, my forehead remarkably moist, my mouth remarkably dry.

I flipped to the dust-jacket notes. They were not encouraging. They said Norman Sherry, a Fellow of the Royal Society of Literature, had researched Greene's life by travelling to "spectacular" sites like Haiti, Argentina, Paraguay, Japan, Malaya, and Sierra Leone. He had been blinded for six months and had fought off fever in Africa and gangrene in Panama. Oh yes, and Ken Rockburn hadn't even read his book.

I buzzed the receptionist and asked her to tell Sherry I was preparing the studio and would only be a few moments. I assessed what I knew about Graham Greene, which, I realized quickly, was limited to his novels. I knew nothing of his life. I took a deep breath, closed my eyes, and opened the book at random. When I looked down, I saw a passage describing Greene's wish to transcend the limitations of his class and his endless fascination with conflicted middle-class people who had fallen from grace. It was all I had to go on.

I escorted Norman Sherry to the studio and we joked about the case of mistaken identity. He seemed a very pleasant and amiable man.

As the tape machine in the studio began rolling, I mentally crossed my fingers and asked, "Norman Sherry, about a third of the way through your book you describe Graham Greene as being a man who was drawn towards people he was not likely to find in the upper classes he came from, a man intrigued by those who have fallen from grace. Is this the key to his personality?"

His face lit up. "That's very astute of you," he said.

Twenty minutes later I thanked him and we brought the interview to a close. It had been lively and entertaining and quite possibly one of the most interesting pieces I had done in some time.

And it was all due to Norman Sherry's enthusiasm for his subject.

When Sherry and I reached the front door of the radio station, he took my copy of the book from me, pulled out a pen, and scribbled something in it. Then he thanked me again, said he hoped to see me with Volume Two, and left.

As I made my way back to my office, feeling something less than astute, I almost couldn't bring myself to look at what he had written. I was convinced my sham had not worked and Sherry, being the gentleman he was, had let me save face.

When I got the nerve to sneak a look, here is what I found:

> For Ken Rockburn on the occasion of our interview together (in spite of the green fertilisers!). You are an awfully stimulating interviewer.

I swore right there I would read Volume Two even if I never saw Norman Sherry again.

❏

In Aldous Huxley's *Brave New World* there is a game called the "centrifugal bumblepuppy." It involves rolling balls down a cone-shaped structure to the bottom, then starting over again. It is a game with no point, played only for the mindless diversion it afforded.

Broadcasting, particularly radio, often feels like a never-ending game of centrifugal bumblepuppy. You work hard at something, give it your best shot, and it's dispersed out into the ether never to be seen or heard again; you have no idea if anyone absorbed it, if it made a difference to anybody's life, if it mattered at all.

This used to bother me until I realized it was actually a mani-festation of radio's success, or at least what used to be radio's success. Most of us take radio for granted, the way we sometimes take our friends for granted. Radio is just there, on in the background usually, and when you're paying attention to it, listening to a good broadcaster like a Peter Gzowski or an Arthur Black, it's like having an intimate, one-sided conversation with a close friend; you don't think to let them know that you're fond of them, or agree with them or appreciate them, because they'll be back tomorrow or next week, saying something different. They're always there.

I've had old friends whom I haven't seen in years return to live in Ottawa and not call me up because they hear me so frequently on the radio they unconsciously begin to think that they are in touch with me. When you work in television — as I do now — it is no real surprise when people on the street recognize you. Yet for most of my broadcasting career I worked on radio, and I never ceased to be amazed at the number of strangers who recognize you by the sound of your voice, and who feel like they know you well enough to speak to you as if you were an old friend. When this happens, it makes all of those endless hours sitting alone in a small studio, talking into a microphone, wondering if anybody was listening, worthwhile.

If "Medium Rare" was a centrifugal bumblepuppy, it was a pretty good one while it lasted, and what you're going to find in this book are some of its bright spots. I hope it works as well on the page as it did on the air.

Ken Rockburn
Ottawa
March 1995

The
Beat
Angels

For a few days in Quebec City back in 1987 I made the mistake of looking a little too long and a little too hard at one of the myths of my youth. I discovered how cultural icons become covered in illusions like so much lichen on rock.

In those tender years around the age of sixteen or seventeen, one of the biggest influences on me and my friends was the music of Bob Dylan. In the early sixties, living in our parents' suburban homes, it seemed our lives were neatly laid out in front of us the same way our mothers used to lay out each day's clothes at the foot of the bed. So it was intoxicating and tantalizing to listen to this scratchy-voiced poet singing about racism in the south and penniless winter days in big cities, about paying the ConEd bill and talkin' World War Three blues, and about seeing that his grave was kept clean. What made it even better, of course, was that our parents thought he was just awful.

Looking back (something Bob never did), it's embarrassing to realize how contrived and affected Dylan's posturing was, even though most of his work endures. But Dylan also exposed us to the writers and poets of an earlier generation, who helped shape and permanently set our impressionable young minds. We discovered the Beats: Allen Ginsberg, Gregory Corso, John Clellon Holmes, William Burroughs, Lawrence Ferlinghetti, Neal Cassady, and — the Beat Angel to beat all angels — Jack Kerouac.

Kerouac's appeal grew out of the doomed romanticism that swathed his characters like a thick fog. We were too young to realize that these fictional antiheroes were just acting out Kerouac's own feelings of futility and purposelessness in the wake of the Second World War — something my generation knew nothing about — but still, how we longed to be part of it all. We lounged in candle-lit rec rooms wearing jean jackets and cowboy boots, rolling our own cigarettes, picturing ourselves as one of the "sunburned and dirty and wildlooking" characters in *The Dharma Bums*, who "got in the car and drove back to San Francisco drinking and laughing and telling long stories."

The car was the romantic centrepiece of this life. When Sal Paradise and Dean Moriarty piled into theirs in *On the Road*, it was proof cars were more than just a couple of tons of chrome and metal; they were the means of escape, the almost mystical vehicles of redemption that could let you leave the dull and passionless life of the suburbs and roll over uninterrupted highways to newer and shinier places.

I remember the start of one chapter in *On the Road* that captured it all. "What is that feeling when you're driving away from people and they recede on the plain til you see their specks dispersing? — it's the too-huge world vaulting us, and it's goodbye. But we lean forward to the next crazy venture beneath the skies." My God, yes.

Many years later, Bob Dylan and Sam Shepard wrote a song called "Brownsville Girl" and in it was a line about driving a car until the wheels fell off and burned. It was still a powerful image for me.

So in October of 1987, I rolled into Quebec City in my beat-up old Monte Carlo, the way Sal and Dean had rolled into Denver or San Francisco, to meet the survivors of that legendary time thirty-five years earlier.

The reason for the trip was a rencontre, a gathering to examine the French-Canadian roots of Jack Kerouac. The bars and boîtes of the old city were filled with intense young Québécois men puffing on Gitanes and carrying on animated discussions of Kerouac's French-Canadian past; there were plenty of unsmiling, black-clad young women wearing berets and looking like extras in a Roger Corman beatnik thrill-kill movie; and there were some of the central characters — Kerouac's first and best biographer, Ann Charters, poet Lawrence Ferlinghetti, who owns City Lights bookstore in San Francisco, the ubiquitous Allen Ginsberg, and the woman who had married Neal Cassady and had once been Kerouac's lover, Carolyn Cassady.

My first and lasting image of Carolyn Cassady was of her sitting in a large, overstuffed living-room chair in one of the rooms at a youth centre, which functioned as the headquarters of the gathering. She was surrounded by young people bringing her coffee and lighting her cigarettes.

She had first met Neal Cassady at the University of Denver in 1947, so I guessed she was in her late fifties (I later learned she was sixty-three). I had seen pictures of her with Cassady and Kerouac when she was a striking-looking young woman. Now she looked like everybody's mom.

I was intrigued by this modestly dressed and conservative-looking woman who had such a remarkable history with the two central characters of the Beat Generation. She had married Neal, had three children with him, had shared their home with Jack, and had watched the two men go on a wild tear with plenty of drink and plenty of other women. Then she and Jack became lovers, while he still lived in the house and she was still married to Neal.

This was the person who knew both men, if not best, certainly most intimately. There had been other women who had Jack and Neal's attention — especially Neal's — but Carolyn's time with them happened when they were at their peaks and the configuration of the relationship was unique.

So I was taken aback by her assessment of the two men.

"They were like college men I had known before, so I didn't see anything unusual about them," she told me. "Of course, Neal had this intense interest in just YOU, which was rare in any field, any time, anywhere. But Jack was just an ordinary bloke. Just a nice guy."

The late forties and early fifties were not known for the recognition of women as equal members of the culture, yet Cassady said both Neal and Jack treated her with respect.

"The best times we had," she recalled, "were when all of us were sitting around reading Shakespeare or discussing Céline or Spengler, and they'd listen to me and I was part of it, and they were just as interested in my opinion as in their own. I never felt like a victim. I don't know about the other women, but I never felt that way, as far as when we were together. And I think that a lot of people have gotten this wrong because of the stereotypes. I was considered just as important a person as any of their friends."

While that sounded reasonable on the surface, I was struck by something in her voice, something too flip and too casual in the way she talked about "sitting around discussing Céline or Spengler." Carolyn Cassady, I knew, looked good on paper: a graduate from Bennington College and an M.A. in fine arts and theatre arts from the University of Denver. She had already written one book about that part of her life — *Heart Beat*, which was made into a Hollywood film — and was in the process of finishing *Off the Road: My Years with Cassady, Kerouac and Ginsberg*, which would come out in 1990. Yet there was a quality about her that put me in mind of a slightly boozy, not especially bright suburban housewife mixing Valium and white wine in the afternoon while she tries to remember what she learned about Spengler and the decline of western civilization in her German philosophy course.

When I pressed her to evaluate Kerouac's work, that image became even sharper.

"I couldn't understand what all the to-do was about," she said. "In every decade or so, there's the Bohemians, or the Jazz Age, or Picasso, somebody that comes along with some new thing that shakes up the establishment and makes them feel threatened. So why was this all such a big deal?

"I mean I think he's a great writer, although I don't read that kind of book for pleasure," she admitted. "I don't understand this hullabaloo at all — I never have. Of course I could see that Jack was a wonderful writer, that's why I saved all his letters. He was just a brilliant writer. It's just that the subject matter was so depressing to me. It's not the kind of book I read."

Nonplussed by this confession, I went to Allen Ginsberg for his reaction. Ginsberg was Kerouac's fiercest supporter and closest friend next to Neal Cassady. The always gentle and unassuming poet maintained a bemused stance on Carolyn Cassady's bewilderment.

"The other day she heard someone reading stuff aloud from Kerouac and she said, 'gee, I never could read Kerouac, but hearing it read aloud, I liked it,'" he chuckled. "Carolyn has a sort of bourgeois housewife view, a philistine view in some respects. She has a great deal of insight as a friend, as Neal's wife, and as Jack's girlfriend occasionally, but it isn't a literary interest and it isn't a high cultural interest particularly, nor would she say it is. So you have to take that for what it is. You know, a prophet is honoured except in his own family? Kerouac's mother didn't read his work."

I was willing to take Ginsberg's opinion seriously, more seriously than Carolyn Cassady's certainly, but I wasn't sure about his contention that her insights into the two men as a friend were as valuable as he thought.

I decided a third opinion, Lawrence Ferlinghetti's, would be worth soliciting. But getting to the irascible writer proved to be more difficult than I anticipated.

Lawrence Ferlinghetti owns what is arguably the most famous bookstore in North America and he is a poet of some repute, known best for *Coney Island of the Mind.*

On this particular day, Lawrence Ferlinghetti was not in a good mood. He had reason. One of the other old Beat poets attending the gathering was Kerouac anthologist and pamphleteer John Montgomery. Like many of Kerouac's friends, Montgomery had appeared in several of Kerouac's novels under different names. For a couple of days at the conference, Montgomery had circulated among the crowds passing out slips of paper. Each was the same: a page from a mail order catalogue featuring a drawing of an expensive leather bomber jacket. It was described as a "genuine *On the Road* jacket," and beside the picture was a quote from Ferlinghetti. It said if Jack were alive, he'd be wearing one.

To John Montgomery, this was blasphemy of the highest order and he was doing his damnedest to make sure Ferlinghetti was embarrassed beyond words. To make matters worse for himself, Ferlinghetti had worn the offending jacket — "no doubt a freebie," crowed Montgomery — to the gathering. Every time somebody spoke to Ferlinghetti, they would stop, touch his sleeve, and say something like, "Is this the jacket? Verrry nice." He was mortified.

I spotted him off in a corner, being interviewed by a CBC radio reporter, smiling away and nodding while she framed five-minute-long questions. He scowled at me as I approached. Undaunted, I stood a few feet away, waited until he was done, then made my move.

"Mr. Ferlinghetti, could I get just a couple of minutes with you, please?"

"Sorry, I haven't the time."

"C'mon, you made time for the CBC. How about a few seconds for a real working stiff? I promise I won't even mention the jacket."

He glared at me and, after a second or two, said, "Oh, alright. But make it fast."

Lawrence Ferlinghetti appeared quite elderly, bald on top with a fringe of long white hair hanging down past the collar of his expensive, soft-leather, genuine *On the Road* bomber jacket.

To him, Kerouac's drinking and carousing and his spiritual angst were a direct outgrowth of his religious background, something over which Kerouac had no control.

"Jack got it from his French Catholicism strained through Quebec," Ferlinghetti maintained. "The folk catholicism of Quebec, I don't know much about it, but it seems to me that it emphasized the phantoms and the dark side of life, and the suffering. So then Jack was attracted to Buddhism and was transformed from a Catholic into a Buddhist, and he was also attracted by the Buddhist conception of suffering as being the ground of human existence."

This was sounding more like the Kerouac that everybody liked to remember: the supremely talented writer, searching for spiritual meaning, his talent unrecognized or worse, reviled, finding solace in the bottle and the fast life.

But Carolyn Cassady was having none of that noble-minded Buddhist stuff.

"I think his life was an effort to escape," she claimed. "Of course, that's obvious. The Buddhism was an escape. And with the drugs and the alcohol and the escape and the self-pity and the illusions and the disillusions and the whole thing, he was such a typical example of that side of that nature, so sensitive and so easily hurt and so into self-pity.

"Of course, he never was a Buddhist. It was just a way of going off into cloud nine and never having to face reality, and the earthly things that were happening to him.

"Okay, they were interested more in trying to find a spiritual identity. Right. We all went along with that and their experiments in it. But from what I hear and read, the Beat Generation people felt that they had to plumb the very depths of human experience and go through it, and all. But I disagree with that. I think you can transcend from where you are. I mean, good Lord, there's enough people that give you pretty vibrant illustrations of what happens when you degrade yourself — why do you have to go through it?

"And so this great admiration and making heroes out of men who are indulging in their bestiality . . . I won't even say animal nature, because animals are innocent, they don't have the minds that can get to those depths. And these men have been made into heroes, and this is something I just will not understand."

By now, I was beginning to wonder just what there was about this bunch that appealed to anybody. I recalled the savage criticism of Kerouac's work when it was first published and wondered if perhaps some of those critics weren't right after all.

Kerouac's biographer Ann Charters had written that he had been ridiculed for his insistence that his work was a huge epic tapestry in the tradition of Balzac and Proust. Critics and other writers like Kenneth Rexroth, Philip Roth, J. D. Salinger, and John Updike treated him mercilessly. *Time* magazine in 1959 called him "a cut-rate Thomas Wolfe"; a review of *Doctor Sax* in the *New York Times* called the book, "largely psychopathic." Appearing on the David Susskind television show, Truman Capote dismissed Kerouac's work as typing, not writing.

"Really, the stuff you read," Carolyn Cassady told me. "I've got the clippings from newspapers. It was just as though they were hunted animals, their defence was so cruel and so coarse — they were terrified. It was just as though they really were threatened. They thought the whole establishment was going to fall apart, I guess. It was amazing.

"And, of course, it was not anything like Jack wanted or expected or could take. He never got over it."

Allen Ginsberg agreed. I went looking for him and found him showing off a new purchase he had just made, a vinyl car coat he had found in some second-story discount clothing store.

"Look at this," he said proudly, fingering its shiny surface, "just fifteen bucks. This is great."

Ginsberg's coat looked like it had been made out of the front seat of Sal and Dean's car. If Jack were alive, I bet he'd be wearing one, I thought.

I asked Ginsberg what he thought of the critical barrage against Kerouac.

"I think they kind of poisoned the well," he answered. "The image I've often had is that Kerouac had a very open heart and was very vulnerable. He offered his heart to America, and when it was rejected, it was like a lover being rejected.

"He did have a great grasp of American intuition and American style and American potentiality, like Melville, like Whitman. He did prophesy a second religiousness, and a tenderness for America, like Whitman did. And, as Whitman did in his later life, he saw America becoming more and more materialistically oriented, and more and more gross. Whitman said that America may ultimately become among the fabled damned of nations, and I think Kerouac had that same sense of a hardening of the heart of America.

"I remember a conversation in which I asked, what happens if the Cold War gets so bad and the military gets so bad in both countries that there is a war between Russia and America? And he said, 'I'd commit suicide. It would be like Dostoyevsky fighting Herman Melville.'"

Whitman, Melville, Dostoyevsky, Spengler: the big questions and the big answers, but especially the big questions — this was what Kerouac and Cassady and Ginsberg and all of these people were supposed to be about, wasn't it? But all it took was another conversation with Carolyn Cassady to make it sound like just another TV soap opera, but with classier literary references.

"Obviously Allen had a sexual competition thing," she said, dismissing Ginsberg with a wave of her hand. "I understand that, just as if he were a woman. The only thing I think is fairly interesting is that these men don't care. They don't respect me as a person, and, at least from what I get from them, I am not worth talking to or bothering about."

But wait. Wasn't this the same woman who told me that Jack and Neal treated her like an equal? Was she saying the rest of the Beats were misogynists?

She told me a story to prove her point.

In 1980, Hollywood made a film version of Carolyn's first book, *Heart Beat*. It starred Cissy Spacek as Carolyn, Nick Nolte as Neal, and John Heard as Jack. Director John Byrum took liberties with the book, and the final product was described by one critic as more fiction than fact. Several of Jack and Neal's friends held Carolyn responsible.

"They all said I'd sold them down the river for mountains of cash," she complained. "Nobody ever talked to me about it. I had written these poison pen letters all summer long to this director and writer, because I had no more control over it, trying my damnedest to change this thing. And for some reason, I don't know why, Allen happened to read those letters and he telephoned me from Boulder and said, 'I had no idea you'd gone through this.' And I thought, why the hell don't you talk to me?

"I love Allen," she went on, "and we've had a long history together. We're very different, but I like where he's coming from. I'm so happy that he's gotten what he wants, even if it's not something I'd do. I'd just really like to be friends with him."

By the late sixties, while Jack worked on ending his life with alcohol in his hometown of Lowell, Massachusetts, and at his mother's house in St. Petersburg, Florida, Neal was busy achieving his own legendary status as the driver of Ken Kesey's "Merry Pranksters" bus. That final chapter of Neal's life, which ended in a drug and alcohol overdose beside some railroad tracks in Mexico, was chronicled in Tom Wolfe's book *The Electric Kool-Aid Acid Test*.

I was beyond any sense of surprise when Carolyn said, "Tom Wolfe didn't understand Neal at all.

"Poor Tom, he just couldn't possibly understand this weird man, especially where Neal was then. So whatever he says in that book is really kind of off-the-wall — it's coming through Tom Wolfe, but it really wasn't very close to the man I knew. And Ken [Kesey] said he didn't like the book either."

By this time I was left with only one question that nobody could answer: if Carolyn Cassady was — at best — a judgemental, uptight matron who never had any interest in the issues that apparently consumed the lives of Kerouac and Cassady, and both of these men found her appealing, what did this say about them? Was it possible that they were just a couple of self-indulgent college seniors who lucked into a literary sensibility that became popular?

After all, by the end of their days they weren't even speaking to each other: Kerouac became an alcoholic anti-Semite who couldn't break free from his mother's apron strings; and Neal Cassady turned into a superannuated hippie who wanted to take every drug, empty every bottle, and sleep with every woman he met.

Certainly there weren't a great many admirable forces at work over the years in the relationships between all of the central figures — alcoholism, sexual promiscuity, homosexual jealousy, satyrism, egomania, anti-Semitism. The image of the once robust Kerouac reduced to a paunchy, weeping lush phoning Carolyn — the woman who would come to both vilify and deify him — in the middle of the night, pleading for understanding, is not a replenishing one.

Yet writers of influence and genius have deteriorated before (Hemingway springs to mind) and will deteriorate again (it is likely happening to Dylan right now), but it should not affect how their previous work is judged. Jack Kerouac's books, in particular *On the Road*, are valuable and important because of the fresh, new writing they contain. Kerouac's "spontaneous prose" seems to pour off the page into your head like quicksilver. I still remember the first time I read Sal and Dean's story; it seemed to gallop along dragging me with it at breakneck speed, barely giving me time to inhale. When I later learned that he had written it in three weeks on rolls of paper, almost nonstop on coffee and pills (prompting the Truman Capote remark), I wasn't the least bit surprised. It read that way and it was meant to be read that way.

So for a decade, from the late forties to the late fifties, Kerouac's writing — and the music of Charlie Parker, the painting of Jackson Pollock, and the photography of Robert Frank — offered up a vision. It told of a hunger for life experience, an attempt to find answers in the full-tilt boogie of living.

At the time it was heady and exhilarating. But my mistake, the same mistake made by many others, was to believe that the philosophy could be taken out of its time and still be valid.

In Quebec City in 1987, I tried to pick it up in both hands and hold it up to the light to admire it. I discovered that it had "best before 1959" stamped on the bottom and you could see daylight through the holes in it.

As I drove down Highway 40 on my way home that autumn afternoon, I could still hear Carolyn Cassady's words.

"I didn't realize until just recently that I did have something in common with them," she told me, "in that our dissatisfactions with the war and the slaughter and stuff, you know, there was something missing in life. We did have that in common, but to find out it was a movement and a *generation* . . . I still don't understand. The trouble is I don't care all that much."

2
Take Off
Your
Thirsty
Boots

Before there was rock, there was folk. By the late fifties, as the bebop culture of Kerouac, Cassady, Ferlinghetti, and Ginsberg began to fade, a new generation started looking to folk and blues music again. A young Bob Zimmerman journeyed from Hibbing, Minnesota, to New York City to visit his ailing idol, the legendary Woody Guthrie. In Cambridge, Massachusetts, hub of more university campuses than you could count, coffeehouses and folk clubs began to spring up. Young, aspiring musicians put away their Charlie Parker albums and began listening to The Weavers and Woody and Pete Seeger, then moved on to singers like Bukka White and Sleepy John Estes and Bill Munroe.

"There was a very active local scene," folkie Tom Rush once joked to me. "Young English majors like myself, who thought the blues were terrific and hoped that we too, when we grew up, could be convicts or field hands, something with some grit to it."

The folk revival was on, and it wasn't long before it swept its way into Canada. In my hometown, Ottawa, one of the most enduring and well-known coffeehouses in all of North America was born: Le Hibou — the owl. Although it changed locations at least three times in its existence, Hibou, as we casually called it, was always the focal point for what was happening musically through the entire decade of the sixties. It was a key link in a chain of clubs that reached across Canada to Vancouver, down the coast to San Francisco, back across the States to New York City. Everybody who was anybody played at Hibou, from the Chicago blues greats like Muddy Waters and Otis Spann, to the delta blues of Mississippi John Hurt and Sonny Terry and Brownie McGhee. And the "neo-folkies" too, those English majors who were so much like us, came through — John Hammond, Tom Rush, Eric Andersen, the Jim Kweskin Jug Band with Maria Muldaur, Tom Paxton, Gordon Lightfoot, a very young Joni Mitchell, the list went on and on.

Changing musical tastes and higher operating costs forced Le Hibou into oblivion in the early seventies, but memories of those fine days stayed permanently fixed in the minds of me and my friends. So much so that two and a half decades later, with a free-wheeling radio program at my disposal, I indulged my nostalgia and tracked down a number of those old "neo-folkies" for a chat. The results were sometimes satisfying, sometimes mystifying, and, at least once, aggravating.

Let's start with that one.

❏

Sometimes, no matter how hard you try and how ingratiating you can be, you come up against a personality that just cannot be won over.

Such was the case with Ramblin' Jack Elliot.

Here was a figure who loomed large in the mythos of my youth: the man upon whom Bob Dylan based his early persona; a mythical figure who hung out with Woody Guthrie; a man who, despite his upbringing, affected the guise of the rootless cowboy so successfully he came to believe it himself. In reality, he was Elliot Adnopoz, a kid from Brooklyn, a student at a Connecticut private school, who just wanted to be a cowboy and ran away from home to make his dream come true.

To this very day, when I think of Ramblin' Jack, I see the picture that graced his record *Bull Durham Sacks & Railroad Tracks*: Jack, in cowboy hat and denims, hands on hips, legs planted firmly apart, that cowboy-handsome face gazing off into the distance.

In 1991, Jack showed up at the Mariposa Folk Festival in Toronto. He was scheduled to play several workshops and performances over two or three days, including one with another folk legend, Dave Van Ronk.

I sat up front, snapping pictures of the two men as they muddled their way through several tunes and told endless stories — rambling, you might say — about the times they hung out with Bob Dylan. Old Jack was just that: old. I figured he must be in his early sixties; he was wearing wire-frame glasses and was looking a tad on the grizzled side.

After the concert, I approached him backstage and suggested that since we were staying in the same hotel, perhaps we could get together for an interview later that evening. "Sure thing," he enthused. "Listen, I've only had a couple of hours' sleep. Let me go back and have a nap. You call me in my room around seven and we'll do it then."

Satisfied that all was arranged, I went and took in a few more concerts.

At seven that evening I called his room. "Look," he said, "I got waylaid by some friends this afternoon and didn't get to sleep. How about we leave this 'til tomorrow morning?"

I reluctantly agreed. "Where'd you say you were from again?" he asked. I told him. "Hey, Le Hibou! Man, that was one of my favourite houses to play. Owned by Harvey Glatt, right?"

I said, yes, Harvey Glatt did own the defunct folk club at one point. And Harvey, I added, trying to ingratiate myself to him, was also the guy who owned the radio station I worked for.

"No kidding," he said. "Say, I've got stories about Harvey." And for the next forty minutes he told me tales of his stays in Ottawa, his life on the road, the people he knew. Finally, we agreed to get together at ten o'clock the next morning in his room. "I've got to get some sleep tonight," he pleaded.

As I hung up I had the uneasy feeling that that phone conversation was the only interview I was going to get. I shrugged it off and headed for the bar in the hotel basement.

About an hour later, I looked up from my conversation with a friend at the bar to see Jack strolling in, his arm around the shoulders of one of the young women who drove the shuttle bus between the hotel and the festival site, a woman young enough to be *my* daughter.

"Where can I get a bottle of Jim Beam?" he asked the woman tending bar.

When told he couldn't, he muttered, "Damn," and left with his friend.

"The old goat," the bartender said to me. "He was in here last night, too." I seriously began to doubt that Jack would be in his room at ten the next morning.

Sure enough, when I made the call there was no answer. I checked the performance schedule and saw that Jack was due to play at two o'clock that afternoon on the main stage with several other folkies. I made my way to the site and prepared to ambush him during his sound check, which I assumed would be at least half an hour before the start of the show. Two minutes before the set was due to begin, a golf cart driven by a festival worker careened up to the side door of the stage carrying Jack, guitar case in hand and cowboy hat at a rakish angle.

I walked up to him. "Hey, Jack."

He turned and looked at me blankly.

"Ken, remember, from Ottawa?"

"Oh. Yeah."

"So I phoned you this morning at ten, but you weren't in your room."

"Sure I was," he said. "Sure I was. I didn't hear any phone."

This was not going well. "Jack, no kidding, I called. But look, what about the interview, when can we do it?"

"Well now, I was thinking about that," he said, his tone turning colder as he leaned towards me. "I don't see why I should bother doing any interview" — he bore down on the word like he had just found a dead mouse at the bottom of a bottle of Jim Beam — "when there ain't no house for me to play in Ottawa. Right? I mean, what good is it for me to do an interview for a city that I can't even play in?"

I realized from the fumes coming off him that his revels from the night before were not quite over, but I was too mad to care.

"Look, you promised me an interview and you've put me off twice already. Are you going to do it or not?"

His toughness wilted like a time-lapse film of a dying flower. "Say, what about this," he said. "How about you come up on stage with me? There's like six or seven guys playing, so you can interview me between my turns."

"What, are you crazy?" I was losing it very quickly. "Do an interview while you're performing? Don't be an idiot."

Good Lord, I remember thinking, *I've just called one of the heroes of my youth an idiot.*

"Wait a minute . . . just wait . . . I'll check it out," he muttered as he turned and scurried through the stage door. Moments later one of the festival organizers came out, walked up to me, and said, "Look, Jack can't do any interviews now, he's about to go on stage. Give the guy a break, will you?"

I could only stand there and sputter. The old goat.

❒

Not long ago I came across the movie version of "Alice's Restaurant" late at night on one of those high-number television channels that seem to show only old, bad movies. What a painful experience. Made in 1967, the movie was a rendering of Arlo Guthrie's very funny signature song of the same name. But the

film, in which Guthrie played a central role, was burdened with
flat, dreadful acting, an embarrassing, terminally hippie earnest-
ness, and a complete lack of humour. "Alice's Restaurant," the
song, had been a joyful, good-natured poke at a society that
blithely sent its young men off to die in a war — Vietnam — that
not many of them really believed in.

In 1988 I met Arlo Guthrie at the Mariposa Folk Festival and,
sitting in the middle of a field on the grass away from the noise
of the concert stage, he told me that he had quit doing the song
when the war ended in 1972, had not performed it until its
twentieth anniversary in 1987, and hadn't done it again since. He
said that between 1967 and 1972, the song was always current
and topical, but once the war was over, he didn't want it to
become a sentimental, nostalgic number that he felt he had to
perform at every concert.

Arlo Guthrie is a man who lives in the shadow of his famous
father in more ways than one. To decide to pursue the same line
of work as your father, when he is a man the stature of Woody
Guthrie, is at the same time both understandable and brave. Yet
Arlo has managed to carve out his own career while living com-
fortably with his dad's looming legend. Even more ominous,
though, is the spectre of Huntington's chorea. The disease that
killed Woody is hereditary and can easily, but not always, attack
the next generation. It has not affected Arlo into his forties.

Arlo Guthrie grew up surrounded by music and musical giants.
As a kid he remembers being babysat at the Newport Folk Festival
by a very young Bob Dylan. "I remember my mom put him in
charge of me, saying, 'okay, take our Arlo and don't let him
wander around!'" Guthrie smiled at the memory. "I must have
been about fourteen or fifteen and I remember going around with
Bob and he's saying, 'Hey, this is Woody's kid!' And I recognized
that the way people were looking at him, the way people were
responding to him, that he was an important person. I wasn't
quite sure why — I knew it had something to do with music or

what he was writing about — but I was still too young to be his friend or his buddy, or something like that. I was just a kid."

When the Vietnam War ended and the folk boom died, Arlo Guthrie kept right on singing and playing. He often logs in upwards of two hundred nights a year on the road, travelling in a large tour bus with fellow band members, friends, and family. His audiences tend to be a cross section of people, he told me. "About a third of my audience is my own peers, people who have been coming to see me for years. There's a whole 'nother third of young people who are showing up. Now, they know the words to all this stuff. So maybe there's a revival of interest in not just me but some of the things that have to do with the sixties. There are a lot of kids who are running around, who are the same people who would go to the Dead concerts or something like that, who are showing up at my shows, and I'm real happy about that. And then there's a third who's just sort of a mixture of grandmas, and people who come from my father's generation, just people who are interested in who's coming through town."

A great deal of Guthrie's appeal comes from the same source as his father's: he seems to understand aspects of the human condition that cut across generational boundaries. "My own perception of what's real has so drastically changed since I was a kid, and yet in some ways it hasn't changed at all," he said. "I remember being eighteen and saying to myself and to other people, 'I know this isn't all there is. I don't know what else there is, but I know this isn't all of it right here.' The daily grind of going to school and getting a job and getting an education, or going to college or getting a spouse and some kids and a nice little house and a white picket fence, *there's got to be more!* So I suspect that there's a lot of young kids who know that there's more to get. They're not exactly sure, like I wasn't sure, what it is or how it fits or whether it can be thought of in a nice little easy-to-understand formula — which there isn't. So the questions are the same, they're always the same: *what's real? what am I doing here? how come I don't understand it, or how come I think I do? how come, when I think I do, something always goes wrong and screws it up again?* Those kinds of questions are always legit."

Not surprisingly, Guthrie also has a sophisticated understanding of what constitutes a political song that has enough appeal to last for decades. "The songs that are still sung that have great meaning," he explained, "are generally simple songs. They don't detail events so much as that they are able in a very, very simple way, almost a childlike way, to mean more than they are. 'If I Had a Hammer,' perfect example. 'Blowing in the Wind,' perfect example. These are songs that are sung at every little kids' camp, they're sung in schools, they're sung in churches, they're sung at festivals, they're sung everywhere. That's because they don't necessarily mean what they say, or they mean something else. To a kid singing at a camp, it's just a fun song to sing that makes sense. To a spirited performer who's playing it to an audience of inmates somewhere, some of that stuff means a little more. And to the extent that we understand and participate in the event that's going on, whether it's a political event, a social event, or anything like that, it takes on a different life.

"And, hopefully," he added, "those songs will be around for a long time, but you can't write them with names of people or with events. My dad wrote a million songs like that — they're not sung anymore. Everybody says, 'how come your dad's songs are still around?' Those songs that he wrote about specific events are not around! That's the point. The 'This Land Is Your Land'-type of song, that just in a general way says something that anybody can sing, anybody can put their own meaning to — those are the songs that last."

❐

Judy Collins is one of those folk artists whose legacy is having brought other important songwriters to prominence. In that way she is very much like Tom Rush. Although Rush has always claimed that he tried and failed to get Judy Collins to record two songs, "Circle Game" and "Urge for Going," written by a then unknown young songwriter named Joni Mitchell. Collins, he said, just "wandered off." A year or so later, Judy Collins was to have her first commercial hit with another Mitchell song, "Both Sides Now."

In 1966 Judy Collins released an album called *In My Life*. Not only did it offer a poignant version of that well-known Beatles tune, but it also served up material from an impressive array of other new writers: Leonard Cohen, Randy Newman, and Donovan. The record also included the music of Jacques Brel and Bertolt Brecht. It led many of its listeners down paths they didn't know existed.

"It was a very important album for a lot of reasons," Collins told me. She had come into the studio for an interview while in Ottawa playing her cabaret show of Brel and Sondheim songs at the National Arts Centre. She had arrived looking cool and aloof, dressed in a pale-coloured but very business-like suit, accompanied by her publicist and assistant. But this frosty exterior could not reduce the effect of those eyes, those piercing blue eyes that captured the hearts of young men like myself. They had stared off the covers of a series of record albums in the sixties, and had driven Stephen Stills to write one of his most memorable songs, "Suite: Judy Blue Eyes."

"*In My Life* was a kind of gathering together of the things that I had done when I was younger. I was trained as a pianist, I grew up in a very musical household, but I was trained as a pianist in a popular musical household. And then, after playing Mozart in public with a symphony orchestra — I wasn't paid, I was only thirteen so they didn't pay me — at that point I started playing guitar and doing folk music and traditional things. *In My Life* was the breakaway from traditional music and music written by Americans or people purporting to have folk roots."

Collins said the record brought together all of these dramatic and intense lyrics, like Leonard Cohen's "Dress Rehearsal Rag." It featured some of her own writing, broke new ground by using an orchestra, and forced her to begin playing the piano again in order to do songs like "Pirate Jenny" ("who could ever learn those chords on the guitar? I couldn't, maybe Joni Mitchell could — she *probably could* — but I couldn't!").

Easily the most popular track off of the record was Cohen's "Suzanne." "The song is a terrific song," Collins stated simply. "I never wrote any songs. All I knew was singing material that was written by others, from Mozart and Debussy to Leonard Cohen and Pete Seeger and Kurt Weill, and that is a grand and fine tradition in which I was trained, thank the Lord. So my idea of finding the right song had to be very much a match, a perfect match. Otherwise I couldn't do it and, because I didn't do any of my own writing, the perfect matches were made by some hand, not mine."

This hint of divine intervention or otherworldliness appeared again when I asked Collins if she could explain her criteria for picking the right songs to record. "That's very mysterious," she answered slowly, choosing her words. "Better not to try to analyze it, I think, for myself. I listen to an awful lot of material, but the ones that I'm supposed to sing somehow get to me. I don't know exactly how, but they do. Probably I'm supposed to do more and more of my own writing, because I'm finding less and less interesting to sing of other people's."

She said she will listen only to material brought to her by people that she trusts. "If I get something in the mail," she added, "I seldom listen unless they're vetted by someone who's heard them. I don't listen to everything that comes through the mail, and, in fact, you're told by your lawyers not to accept unsolicited material because you can get sued! People will hear a word that's in their song and decide it was their word!"

Collins was blunt about the pivotal points in her career that allowed her to maintain her traditional audience and broaden its scope. She said *Wildflowers*, the follow-up album to *In My Life* that featured the Joni Mitchell–written hit "Both Sides Now," moved her into the mainstream pop area. Her subsequent recording of the traditional religious song "Amazing Grace" brought in a fundamentalist audience. "It reached a lot of people who weren't reached either by the pop market or by the folk market." She then added an older, middle-of-the-road, Frank Sinatra-ish audience when she began recording Stephen Sondheim songs, such as "Send In the Clowns."

"In recent years I've added another dimension to the audience because of the children's work that I've done." She laughed. "Now, of course, I hope they all bond together as one large demographic, running out and buying Judy Collins albums!"

It would be less than a year from this conversation that Bill Clinton would sweep George Bush out of the White House, announce that Judy Collins was one of his and Hillary's favourite singers, and invite the chanteuse to appear at his inauguration festivities. Reports even had the two of them jogging together. Not having any prescient abilities myself, I asked Collins if, after so many years on the road, sometimes she wearied of the work and wished she could put it aside for good.

"Certain parts of it you do," she answered. "You want to concentrate on one thing more than another. At this point I'm doing more writing than I've ever done, both prose and music. But, on the other hand, I have an allegiance to a craft that I do, and so I do work at it and, I think, get better at it as the years go by. That's what I wanted to do. That was my intention."

❐

One of the more entertaining aspects of the folk boom of the early sixties was the Jim Kweskin Jug Band. The ragtag bunch of musicians out of the Cambridge area played their ditzy ragtime and jug band tunes mostly for laughs and, up to 1968 when they broke up, were a welcome counterpoint to the generally sombre and serious themes that prevailed in folk music.

So when I visited the band's former female singer, Maria Muldaur, in her backstage dressing room after a blistering out-door concert in the late eighties, I was only partly startled by what I found. Maria D'Amato had been the only woman in a band comprising Jim Kweskin, Geoff Muldaur (later her husband), Fritz Richmond, a harmonica player named Mel Lyman, Richard Greene, and Bill Keith, who later joined Ian and Sylvia.

The band's demise in 1968 was prompted in large part by the peculiar personality of Mel Lyman, who purchased a hilltop house in Boston and began his own quasi-religion, the Fort Hill Community, with its own newspaper, the *Avatar*, and convinced many of his followers that he was God. While Kweskin himself was involved briefly with the group, the Muldaurs and other band members chose to pass. In later years *Rolling Stone* and other publications would carry stories on the descent of Lyman's group into drug-addled, wacko-cult hell.

Maria Muldaur had modest commercial success over the years, a sort of low-level consistent following that allowed her to keep recording contracts with various small labels. Her biggest success came in the early eighties with "Midnight at the Oasis," from her album *Waitress in a Donut Shop*. Her sultry and bendable voice was always distinctive and appealing, and she showed it off to great effect at the concert I had just witnessed.

I was ushered into her dressing room by her assistant, a pleas-ant, chubby woman in unflattering black lycra tights, a mountain of brittle, blonde beehive hair, and way, way too much makeup. Muldaur was sitting on a couch wearing the same flower-print dress and high heels she had worn during her performance. Her hair was still jet black, and she sounded as youthful as she did in the sixties, but she obviously hadn't turned away too many second helpings over the years. As we were introduced, a tinfoil-covered tray with cold cuts, fruit, cheese, and pastries was carried into the room and placed on a table behind me. Throughout our entire conversation, Muldaur's eyes would disconcertingly wander past my shoulder to that tray.

I had seen the Kweskin Jug Band at Le Hibou in 1967. I remembered the evening because Maria Muldaur had made an onstage remark about James Brown and, when there was no response from the audience, began to berate Ottawa. She burst into loud and long laughter when I reminded her of the story. "What did I do, make 'em feel like a bunch of hopeless squares? The Jug Band was really into roots music and black music and James Brown was hardly an obscure figure in American music, so I guess I was just incensed and thought it was their loss if they didn't know who he was."

Despite the messy business with Mel Lyman, Muldaur claimed that her memories of the sixties were still good. "Number one, the sixties was a great time. It was a time with a lot more artistic freedom, a lot more discovery, things on the music scene were a lot newer. You could have not too much money and still live a nice lifestyle if you were inventive and imaginative enough. Nowadays, you've got to be rich just to be poor, you know what I mean?"

She echoed some of Arlo Guthrie's sentiments. "Kids don't have the chance when they come out of high school to take a year or two off and try to figure out who they are and what life's all about. It's like right away, *make money, make money, make money*. The eighties are very materialistic and the sixties weren't, and there was a lot of idealism. And that's where I live, you know? Both on the political and social scene, as well as the musical scene, it was a wonderful time."

Jim Kweskin and Mel Lyman notwithstanding, Muldaur maintained that the Jug Band was very democratic with no one leader. "And, in those days, you didn't just come in and do a one-nighter — you came to Ottawa or Toronto or wherever you were, and you stayed for two weeks. So you really got to know a town and make friends and know where the good restaurants were and go hear other people jam. We were trying to bring a type of music that wasn't getting played on the radio, early American blues and roots music, and we were doing it jug band style. We'd even do Duke Ellington pieces — the fact that we'd dare to do 'Mood Indigo' with jug band instrumentation was quite crazy of us, but we did it anyway!"

Muldaur, perhaps over-optimistically, felt that there was a resurgence of interest in what she called roots music and blues. She based the claim on the reactions she got from audiences at her concerts. "The blues number always just makes people jump to their feet, and this is a recent thing. In the last couple of years people are recognizing the power of the blues again, whereas I've loved it all along. So that's why I say to them, 'you like the blues? Well, you can take your sissified, pantywaist English anorexic MTV-kind of music, and you know what you can do with it!' And the audience goes 'YEEEAAAHHHH!!!!' Because people are sick of that plastic stuff. It'll just take you so far, but the blues are universal and timeless and this is their hour."

We chatted about the music of New Orleans and her admiration for Aaron Neville and then we shook hands and said goodbye. As her assistant led me out of the dressing room, I glanced back to see Maria Muldaur descending on the food tray with a ravenous look in her eye. The blues, apparently, can also whip up an appetite.

❏

The most enduring songs of the folk era, like those of rock, are the anthems. While the tendency is to associate anthems with political statements, it's not always the case. Certainly "Hey Jude" by the Beatles is not political, but it is definitely an anthem. The same applies to Bruce Springsteen's "Born To Run," while his "Born in the U.S.A." is completely political. In folk, as Arlo

Guthrie so rightly pointed out, the simple songs of his father and Bob Dylan were the ones that fit the anthem description — and one unlikely love song came from a quiet and gentle singer who can still move audiences with it even today. The singer is Tom Paxton and the song is the lovely farewell tune, "That Was the Last Thing on My Mind."

I met Tom Paxton in the lobby of the high school around the corner from my house. He had driven eight hours from New England with his wife to play to a small but very appreciative audience in the school's auditorium. An amiable man with a bushy moustache and cloth cap covering his widening baldness, Paxton spends much of his time travelling and singing in just such venues. He also makes a decent living recording children's songs and marketing his material, like his friend Tom Rush, through a wide mailing list of devoted followers. Paxton's recent albums also contained plenty of Canadian musicians: Dennis Pendrith, Ken and Chris Whitely, Kathryn Moses, and Colleen Peterson.

As we sat on a school bench, Paxton tuning his guitar, I asked him how aware he was of the significance of that one song on so many people. "You're always hearing people say showbiz things like 'it makes me feel so humble!' But it *does* make me feel humble," he answered. "Because it's almost as if I had nothing to do with that song. I wrote it down, that's all. I just wrote it down. I took dictation, and that's the way I feel sometimes. It's almost as if it doesn't belong to me . . . although, I hasten to add, I cash the cheques," he laughed. "I wrote it in 1964. It had absolutely nothing to do with my life as I was living it at the time. I was perfectly happily married — still am to the same woman. It was just a kind of a song that came out, a 'how would I feel if?' kind of song. I'm gratified to see that younger kids know it as well. That makes me very happy — it seems to have been kind of absorbed."

Paxton had a typically disarming reason for the success of folk music. "It's still a great way to meet girls." He grinned broadly.

"That's why a lot of us got started, although perhaps we weren't in touch with those reasons. But, sure, learning how to play a guitar, when you're young, learning how to play a guitar fast and loud. Yeah, that's a good way to meet girls and you might actually turn out to be a musician after all."

Paxton was clearheaded about his glory days in the sixties, describing his feelings about that period with the same intelligent turn of phrase that makes him a good songwriter. "I have very fond memories of those days," he told me, "which is quite different from saying I pine for those days. I don't at all. I pine for tomorrow. I look for tomorrow. I'm enjoying this day. I had to drive up here, a long, long drive, with my wife. We're apart so much of the time — we work in separate places, so we really have to struggle to be together. So we were in the car talking all the way, we talked and talked. So this is a good day. And I've got a concert to do here for some good people. I remember what somebody said about nostalgia, he said it's okay to look back, as long as you don't stare. I do know people who want to talk about nothing but the good old days, and that gets very boring."

Still, Paxton does feel a sense of history, a sense of carrying on a troubadour tradition with his work, something he said he does very consciously. "I think of people like Woody Guthrie — whom I never met — and Pete Seeger, the Weavers. I think of Burl Ives, who I only met once in the elevator in Harrod's in London. There is this tradition of balladeering in the Anglo-Saxon heritage which I come from. So I see myself as one more proponent of that. I'm not a traditionalist, obviously when you hear my music, and I do draw from sources outside — some of my songs I steal from music-hall, some inspiration or influence comes from people like Tom Lehrer, Jacques Brel. I think you remain open to things, which means you're available to love new songs when you hear them and those songs, in a certain, mysterious way, kind of go into the boiler room and eventually come out as one of your own songs, with your own stamp upon it. And yet, if you stand apart from it, you can look at it and say, 'Oh yeah, I would never have written that song if I hadn't listened to several Jacques Brel albums and been knocked out by them! That's my Jacques Brel song, I see.' Which is different from saying, 'I'm gonna write a Jacques Brel song.' That's the exciting part of the creative process."

❒

The sixties folk music scene in Canada, of course, also spawned homegrown talent. Gordon Lightfoot and Joni Mitchell took their turns playing Le Hibou. Bruce Cockburn, an Ottawa lad, spent his early days on stage there as a solo act and with various house bands like The Children. And a new and talented young folkie out of Toronto named Murray McLauchlan began making the rounds.

Like Tom Paxton, Murray McLauchlan saw himself as carrying on a tradition, but a fairly recent one: the urban singer/song-writer, best exemplified by Bob Dylan, Phil Ochs, and Eric Andersen. He saw these singers taking the folk idiom and adding another dimension, putting together words and music that became more than the sum of their parts. "I didn't really start writing songs until I became aware that that possibility existed," McLauchlan told me backstage one afternoon before his sound check for an evening concert. He was pale and weak-looking, suffering from the flu. He said he hoped he could make it through our interview without "blowing chunks" and, mercifully, he did.

He took a deep breath and continued. "I don't know if you could call that a tradition. To me, a tradition is something that . . . well, you're Irish-Scottish, or Italian or black, or whatever. I'm not really set in one musical tradition — in fact, quite the opposite. I write in a lot of different veins, particularly now. I've written songs now that have more in common with Harold Arlen or Hoagy Carmichael or Johnny Mercer than they have with Bob

Dylan. I'm also writing pure country and, in some cases, pure humour based on pure country because it's a genre that occasionally needs to be sent up." He grinned weakly. "You don't see enough Ray Stevens songs out there anymore.

"I guess the tradition that I come from, more than any single factor, would be the kind of broadside, balladeer tradition. Where it has to have content, it has to tell a story, it has to have emotional impact, it's not just a simple lyric . . . ," he broke into singsong, "*It's a nice day, we're gonna have a beach party* — not like that."

McLauchlan didn't learn to play piano until he was in his early twenties and he said that, by working hard at it, he achieved a level of competency that allowed him to expand his interests into other areas of music. That was one, but not the only, reason he began developing a taste for the Arlens and Carmichaels and Mercers. "There is an entry level of sophistication that the lyrics to those songs have. They're simple . . . but they're deceptively simple because they carry an undercurrent of intense irony. Even when they're humorous or light, they're still very ironic. And I think there's an age entry level before you kind of *get* that. I don't want to sound exclusionist, but I think it's really true; you don't really understand how clever a song like 'One for My Baby' is until you've been down that particular emotional route once or twice, the late-night blues. Everybody gets them, but when you get older you get them in a special way," he chuckled.

Murray McLauchlan has made a very respectable living for himself over the years as a singer/songwriter, never achieving the major status of some of his earlier contemporaries like Bruce Cockburn, but always there making music and satisfying his fans. He had struck me as an artist who was never willing to abandon his particular vision for the sake of undiluted commercial success, always wanting to make it on his own terms. When I suggested this to him, I joked that I had never seen him in spandex, for instance. A large grin split his face.

"And you'd never want to, believe me! But I would be as happy as the next geezer anytime that the big hit comes along, and occasionally it has, within the confines of this country certainly, come along often enough that I've managed to sell a lot of records over the years. But, you're right, I've never gone after that phenomenon popularly described as 'corporate rock.' That's certainly a reputable way of approaching your work. I have no quarrels with people who do that — it just doesn't happen to be my particular cup of tea. I'm a great believer in the idea that the product at the end of the day is very important and if it doesn't really deal with people in a very direct and communicative way, then you're wasting their time. So if I haven't got anything to say, then I don't feel like I deserve a hit. Maybe I could get a hit and have nothing to say, I don't know. People obviously do it; hit records now are predicated on many different factors, not just the song, not just what it says, not just how it was recorded, not just how it's sung, but on the imaging and packaging that surrounds it. Vis-à-vis Madonna ad nauseam."

McLauchlan's view of the music business in Canada was equally accepting. It is, he explained, made up of two different businesses. "One is the music business that evolves from megainternational acts and a couple of our own that are like that, that tour through the country every so often and just detonate in the marketplace and get all of the promotional dollars and just roar through and then they're gone in-a-haze-of-smoke-and-everybody's-broke. And then there's everybody else. And the everybody else still includes Michael and Margo Timmins or the Rankin Family or Jeff Healey or Kim Mitchell or blah-blah-blah-blah. Some of them make various and sundry forms of living, but the living that they make in comparison to someone like Bryan Adams is paltry. And also the promotion they get in relation to what is accorded to someone who cracks a record internationally is paltry."

3

Ladies and
Gentlemen . . .
the Green Grocer
of Despair

There is a moment in Donald Britain's documentary, *Ladies and Gentlemen, Mr. Leonard Cohen*, when the young Cohen watches a film of himself sleeping and comments on how rare it is that any of us ever get to see ourselves that way. In this age of instant video imagery it's hard to imagine how right he was. But at the time the remark seemed just the kind of slightly askew perspective Leonard Cohen had on life, just the kind of thing I had come to expect from him. It was one of the reasons I liked him. He seemed capable of a charming ingenuousness that had great appeal; it appealed to young women in his love poetry, and it appealed to young men like myself in his other poems:

> I wonder how many people in this city
> live in furnished rooms.
> Late at night when I look out at the buildings
> I swear I see a face in every window
> looking back at me,
> and when I turn away
> I wonder how many go back to their desks
> and write this down.

On the day when I am writing this down, I am watching large, white flakes of snow dropping slowly on the rooftops outside the window of the third-floor room in my house where I work. Even though I have a quiet Frank Morgan tune playing in the background, inside my head Leonard Cohen is singing "Sisters of Mercy." This is not as incongruous as it sounds. The song, and a couple of Cohen's others, were on the soundtrack of Robert Altman's 1971 film, *McCabe and Mrs. Miller*, which featured Warren Beatty as a turn-of-the-century hustler in a snow-covered northern mining town. The film was such a well-crafted mood piece, and Cohen's music was so perfectly matched to it, that it is impossible to this day for me to look at grey, snowy skies and not hear those songs.

In 1966, folksinger Judy Collins released a record called *In My Life*. On it were two Leonard Cohen songs: "Dress Rehearsal Rag" and "Suzanne," the song that was to become most closely identified with him. When *In My Life* was released, Leonard Cohen was still known as a writer, not a singer. It wasn't until the following year that his first album, *Songs of Leonard Cohen*, came out. Its success was virtually assured because of his reputation as a poet and author (*Beautiful Losers* had been published in 1966) and because of the attention paid to his songs on the Collins album.

Cohen contends that he sang "Suzanne" to Collins over the telephone, not long after he had written it. He doesn't own the rights to the song any longer, which he says is the way it should be.

"There's a combination of circumstances which allow a decent piece of work to really move into the world," he told me. "A lot of luck is involved in that — the question of timing is very pertinent. And the sound of the voice as it moves against the other sounds in the world, those things are very chancy. But also the song is very good . . . it's well constructed."

In the mid-eighties, my wife and I were waiting to disembark from a ferry that had taken us from Algeciras in southern Spain to Ceuta in northern Africa. As we lined up with the other passengers to get off, music began playing over the loudspeakers on the deck. Suddenly we were listening to Leonard Cohen singing "Suzanne." It seemed oddly appropriate.

Another time, my wife and I were sitting at a large, round table during a cabaret concert of Cohen's. Three other couples, strangers, were also seated with us listening to him sing. At one point I turned to say something to my wife and realized that the three other women at the table were weeping.

I offer this as evidence that Leonard Cohen has permeated the lives of a great many people in a great many places. His poetry and songs have been, and continue to be, influential. In the early nineties, a wildly divergent group of young singers released a tribute album of Cohen songs called *I'm Your Fan*. In 1993, he won a Juno Award for "Best Male Vocalist," an honour even he accepted with ironic amusement, given his somewhat monotone singing style. During the summer of 1995, a second tribute album, called *Tower of Song*, featured big-name talents like Sting, Elton John, Peter Gabriel, and Billy Joel doing covers of Cohen's material.

And yet . . . after all of these years, I still don't know whether he's any good.

I know that I find his song lyrics clever, and I've always thought his singing voice was interesting in the same way that Bob Dylan's is interesting, but I am more attracted to the poetry of Raymond Carver or Irving Layton or Anne Sexton. When *Book of Mercy* was published in 1984, I found it almost incomprehensible.

I harbour a suspicion, too, that Cohen may have set out to create Leonard-Cohen-the-poet with a certain amount of planning and intent, that his public persona was a very carefully crafted illusion at which he had worked so long and hard, it had become inseparable from his private self.

Cohen had given hints of this in some of his answers to questions I put to him during a lengthy interview in a suite of rooms at the Chateau Laurier Hotel. I asked him why he had decided so early in his life to take on a career that was notorious for its absence of income.

"I was looking through an old photograph album, and there is a picture of me that one of my friends took," he replied. "I was thirteen and I had a cigarette in my lips and I was reclining on a couch sort of like a later photograph of Truman Capote and I wrote under it 'author?' So I've always had this notion that there's something I should do in that realm."

For a publicity questionnaire early in his career, Cohen gave a typical Cohen answer — part smart-ass, part confessor — to explain his reasons for writing poetry: "First I wrote poems so I could sleep with women, then I slept with women so I could write poems, then I refrained from sleeping with women so I could write poems, then I refrained from writing poems so I could sleep with women."

"I'll stand by that," he laughed, when I read it to him. "I don't know what the later developments and turns in that observation might be, but I'd say that at that point it was probably true, yeah."

Yet some critics maintain it wasn't only in his youth that Cohen was motivated by the pursuit of women. They charge that he has been like that all of his life, a kind of erudite Warren Beatty. Author George Woodcock said women in Cohen's work are nonexistent as intellectual beings, leading to a shallowness of feeling in his love lyrics.

"Screw him," was Cohen's grinning response when read the quote. "Where does anybody get off talking about another man's life or behaviour or work with that kind of certainty? That's dogma. It comes out of his anarchist background. He has an affinity for dogma and that kind of writing is totally beside the point."

But there is no denying that much of Cohen's writing involves a fascination with the opposite sex, and the parade of women through his life is not suggestive of a man with an interest in them as intellectual equals.

His record covers have often featured young women as well (though, of course, this doesn't single him out in the pop music business). For example, the picture on the back of his second album, *Songs from a Room*, shows a young, blonde woman in a straight-back chair, wrapped only in a white towel, seated before a small, portable typewriter in a spare, white room with a shuttered window. Through the cracks in the shutter, daylight can be seen. A small cot covered with a blanket is in one corner of the room. The woman is looking to her left, towards the camera, smiling, her fingers on the typewriter keys. In all likelihood the room is Cohen's house on the Greek island of Hydra, the woman probably his girlfriend, Marianna.

I know how I interpreted that picture when I first saw it back in 1968, as we stood on the cusp of liberation: the shutters are closed at midday and the woman is wearing only a towel because she and the taker of the picture have just made love on the cot. He has left the room briefly (to get the camera?) and upon his return finds the woman playfully pretending to be writing at his typewriter. She quite obviously doesn't belong there — there is no paper in its carriage. Oh, those women. What scamps.

The sepia-tinted photograph on the cover of *Death of a Ladies Man*, his most embarrassing album, shows a dishevelled and brooding Cohen slumped in a "long forgotten Polynesian" cocktail lounge booth between two very attractive women, one of whom is identified as "Suzanne." The picture was certainly designed to support the content of both the record and the book of poetry with the same title, but is still a dramatic illustration, deliberate or otherwise, of women as adornment.

I asked him about the early days. "My standard of living was higher," Cohen said. "When I didn't have money, I lived in a beautiful, big white house in Greece with an exquisite Norwegian girl, breathing fresh air, living in sunlight, walking beside the sea. And then, when I started making money, I started living in hotel rooms, and the complications destroyed the vision I had of what I thought was a proper way to live, which I know now was right."

Sitting across from the latter-day Leonard Cohen in a luxurious hotel suite, it was difficult to imagine him in a seaside garret with an exquisite piece of Norwegian furniture — or was that Norwegian girl? — living off fruit and poetry. He was immaculate in his trademark black pinstripe suit, dark shirt, and spit-shined, black wing tips. He languidly chain-smoked unfiltered cigarettes the entire afternoon, using pauses to inhale as theatrical punctuations to his words. Cohen has the dramaturge's keen sense of gesture and word.

He seems at home in hotel rooms, likely because they have been home to him for much of his peripatetic career. In Donald Britain's film he had said he always felt like he was "on the lam" in hotel rooms. He called them sanctuaries: comfortable, anonymous, subtly hostile environments. Looking around his opulent suite, I suggested the only thing anyone could be on the lam from while staying in such a place was an over-zealous investment broker.

He laughed. "This is a better class of hotel now," he admitted. "I feel like they're going to call me to a board meeting in this hotel room. I used to stay in quite different hotels."

Cohen wrote the notes to the songs contained on *The Best of Leonard Cohen* album released in 1975. According to him, "Sisters of Mercy" was written in a hotel room in Edmonton, "So Long, Marianne" was written in the Chelsea Hotel in New York, "Bird on a Wire" in a motel in Hollywood, "Lady Midnight" in the Henry Hudson Hotel in New York, and "Hey, That's No Way To Say Goodbye" in the Penn Terminal Hotel in New York. Even the cover photograph for the record was taken of Cohen in a hotel room in Milan. Ironically the song "Chelsea Hotel" was started in a Miami restaurant and finished in Ethiopia, though presumably in an Asmaran hotel.

Hotels were also the theme of Cohen's first music video in 1984. The CBC produced a half-hour collection of Cohen songs with the title, *I Am a Hotel*. In it the singer moves slowly through a large hotel, one hand in his pocket, the other holding a cigarette, watching the "guests" and "hotel employees" act out the lyrics. Toller Cranston, Anne Ditchburn, and Celia Franca were among the artists playing roles in the video. It also featured Alberta Watson as "Suzanne" and, as the credits coyly put it, "L.C. as the Resident."

"It's based on some songs I'd already written, an attempt to incorporate them into a series of vignettes or stories that had some cohesion one to the other," Cohen explained, a bit self-consciously. "There are some people who like it; in fact, it was chosen as the Canadian entry into the Montreux Television Festival. I'm not sure how firmly I stand behind it. I think maybe for a first try I'll be forgiven." He paused for a second, then added with a smile, "But I don't think it really makes it."

The idea of the hotel as metaphor was Cohen's but, like the final product, he wasn't about to add it to his resume.

"I think it's a terrible title. You know how these things get into the Xerox machine. You innocently utter an idea, and if there are no other ideas around, you find suddenly this is the title of the thing. I think it's an appalling title."

The spiritual rootlessness symbolized by the endless procession of anonymous hotel rooms is just one of Cohen's carefully cultivated proper trappings for the romantic poet image, along with the stylized and unchanging attire and the constant company of young, attractive women.

He even has an impressive collection of anecdotes that he trots out for interviewers. One of my favourites was about rock producer Phil Spector, the "bullets on the floor" story as I like to remember it.

It was 1977, when he was recording the album *Death of a Ladies Man*. It was to be the object of intense ridicule despite such high-profile studio help as Bob Dylan. The album was produced by the legendary and dramatically eccentric Phil Spector, known for his "Wall of Sound" technique.

"Phil Spector came to a concert I gave in Los Angeles," Cohen began. "We had a mutual friend, we were introduced, and I went up to his house. He was very hospitable, except that he locked the doors and refused to let us leave. And the house was about thirty-two degrees, and I only had a tee-shirt on.

"So I said, listen, Phil, since we're locked in here, let's do something. And he said, good idea. So we went to the piano and we started writing some songs together. I wrote the lyrics and he wrote the music. Sometimes I would alter the music, sometimes he would alter the lyrics, or suggest a repetition. He had been trained in the school of hooks, so he thought if you had a good line you should repeat it at least twenty or thirty times.

"In that period of the actual creation of the songs, he was very accessible. Both of us approached the thing in the spirit of generosity. I liked his work very much and he liked mine, and I think the songs are good. The kind of display of power, the necessity for which seized him in the actual recording, is what changed the record into something I couldn't follow."

Cohen was warming up, giving the impression of someone making spontaneous embellishments to a well-worn story.

"Over the next couple of months I would meet with him every night, and we would put these songs together," he continued. "Phil was delightful on a one-to-one basis. He really is a very, very nice guy. Then something happens to him — I've heard this from other people too — when he gets into the studio and there are other people around. Suddenly there are armed bodyguards, there are bullets on the floor, and general madness begins to reign."

(There have been the suggestions over the years that the "general madness" had much to do with the ingestion of certain substances, which altered the perceptions of everybody in the studio, including Cohen.)

"Now, if you have the energy to challenge the thing I suppose you wouldn't have any energy for anything else," Cohen went on. "And I was very interested in getting the music down in the song. But he would take the tapes away every night under armed guard.

"I remember one occasion about three in the morning when he came over to me with a half a bottle of Manischewitz wine in one hand, and a loaded .45 in the other, and he put his arm around my shoulder and he put the muzzle of the gun against my neck and he cocked it . . . ," the dramaturge paused to take a drag on a cigarette. "And he said, 'Leonard, I love you.' I mean, what can you do?" Cohen smiled.

"When the record was finished, at least when the tracks were finished, I had only done what I considered to be reference vocals. He disappeared into hiding with the tapes and refused to let me attend the mixing sessions. The record that came out was with reference vocals buried under his rather brilliant music. I think if those tracks were just remixed there would be a very good record.

"Sometimes I get a tune and I think, yeah, I'd like to work with Phil again. Then I remember the .45. And it wasn't just Phil, I mean there were three or four other guys around with guns and rifles that I challenged finally. Finally I did divert my energy from the project to confronting these macho characters, and challenging them to draw. It just got that crazy.

"I called them on it. There were guys that were carrying guns who were supposed to be protecting something or other, which I could never quite discover. So one night I just got tired and I started insulting them. I said to them, 'what has to be done to you to get you to draw?' I started to go at them. Because I didn't think any of them had the courage to slay me in the studio, so I had to indicate the absurdity of their armament."

This is a good story, no question about it, replete with Cohenisms like "slay me in the studio" and "the absurdity of their armament." But the image of the skinny, tee-shirted poet challenging armed bodyguards smacks of the kind of war story old vets like to repeat, in which major events are contorted to make the storyteller the focus of attention.

Yet the story does offer a glimpse into the life of another figure who has worked hard on his image. Phil Spector's former wife, singer Ronnie Spector, once said Phil became what the media made him. Reclusive oddball, dangerous schizophrenic, troubled genius, they said it all so often he really turned into those things. The comparisons to Cohen seemed to make him so uncomfortable he couldn't even address the issue directly.

"I don't know," he sighed heavily. "My career has been very modest compared to Phil Spector's career. Phil really articulated a certain kind of music at a particular time, and produced little classic after classic. You may dismiss them as irrelevant but I think there is really fine work there, and he had huge audiences. People are still singing those songs. His association with the Beatles produced great work. So you're talking about one of the princes of the scene, and there were tremendous rewards there, a tremendous amount of money and power. I haven't participated in that kind of largesse, so I suppose the influence to change and to be what they call you has been proportionately less."

It may well be true that Cohen has never "participated in that kind of largesse," but his influence is far more widespread and enduring than anything Phil Spector ever created. And that is due almost totally to Cohen's decision, at the age of thirty-two, to make the leap from poetry on the page to poetry with a backbeat.

"I like playing and writing music but I've never really separated the two," he told me, "and I've always kind of heard an invisible guitar going on behind the things that I write. But I don't really ly divide those things up. The music has involved public performance, which is a whole different enterprise and I like doing that too, because the judgement on that is immediate. You know if you've delivered the song — you can tell by looking at the faces in front of you."

The ease of the transition was also helped by his youthful ignorance of the recording business.

"If anybody decides, as I did, to become a singer, not knowing anything about what the music industry was like . . . if somebody came to me with that suggestion today, I'd try to turn them away. But, because I had the advantage of ignorance, it wasn't difficult for me.

"I think the thing that allowed me to do it was that I had so little thought about it," he added. "I started writing these songs, and I knew they were good because I'd sing them to my friends and they liked them. And the songs moved effortlessly into the world. I hardly did anything to promote them. I didn't go on a concert tour for two years after the first record came out. So they were done very innocently and maybe they had that kind of power."

Unlike many other writers and artists I have interviewed, Cohen was open and honest about his fondness for his own early work. Instead of the usual line that early work is embarrassing and the artist can't listen to it, or read it, or even look at it — like movie actors trying to convince people they have never seen their own films — Cohen was refreshingly proud of his early poems and songs.

"Almost all of them can be stood up and sung at concerts," he said. "For a song to last a tour of a hundred concerts you really begin to discern the weaknesses of the work. But some of those early songs stand up. I was looking at the first book that I wrote, poems that I wrote from the age of fifteen to twenty, and some of those even stand up. So, although one likes to think that one moves from strength to strength, that maturity enters into it as a virtue and all of those things, there is something to be said for work that is the same in a writer, something of a certain standard."

It was here, when he spoke of his work, that I began to get a sense of what might be the real Leonard Cohen. This is a man for whom the process is everything, the creation is what is important, and the hucksterism needed to get it across to an audience is something else. He acknowledged that for him the act of writing is a laborious one.

"There are people who write hundreds of thousands of words on top of the refrigerator and it's great, but the amount of time

57

you spend on it is no guarantee of its excellence, and I do work very slowly."

If the key to understanding the real Leonard Cohen, not the artifice he has so skillfully presented to the world, lies in his work, then it becomes important to look at the other major theme that runs through his writing: his religiousness.

Looking back over his work, from the poems "Absurd Prayer" and "Isaiah" to songs like "Story of Isaac" and "Who by Fire," Cohen has exhibited a strong connection to faith and spiritual tradition.

Cohen said he has never had any difficulty using the word "God" because it is a handy phrase that describes concepts that are a lot more unwieldy. He also acknowledged that his 1984 collection of poetry, *Book of Mercy*, was entirely, as he put it, "addressed towards that source." But he displayed a reluctance to place too much emphasis on this as a motivation.

"You either find yourself in a situation in which you have no alternative but to address that absolute source of things, or you don't," he told me. "If you don't, it's fine. There's no special virtue to writing this kind of book as opposed to another kind of book. This is only under the laws of necessity; you can't choose to write a high-minded, moral book or a book of begging, disconsolate appeals. Whatever the book is, it wasn't written from the point of view of a choice. It was written under laws of necessity."

Cohen's songs and poems describe both the joy and the desperation of love, and the "high-minded morality" and the "begging, disconsolate appeals" of religion. That he does this with tremendous effect is without argument, yet in a strangely ironic way his other success — the success of his image — prevents that final connection between the man and his words. Can even his most rabid fan picture Leonard Cohen begging anyone — God or woman, or both — for anything? Can anyone picture him washing the dishes on a Saturday morning in a tee-shirt and jeans?

Early in his career, he described himself as somebody who was down in the trenches, looking up over the top to see who was doing the shooting, while there were other people up in the watchtower looking out over the whole landscape. In *Book of Mercy* he called himself a singer "in the lower choirs, born fifty years ago to raise my voice this high, and no higher."

"It is an acceptance that you have this particular kind of gift, that there are others who have sung much more freely and much more deeply," he explained. "Still, you're willing to take your place in that choir."

Perhaps, I thought, that is the truest thing he has said. He has a gift that has allowed him to have his name appear on a chair in the lower choirs, and, despite the façade he has fashioned so well, his real voice is heard in his work. In 1985, he wrote a poem on his Greek island retreat of Hydra called "Days of Kindness." I first read it in 1994. It seemed to me I was hearing Leonard Cohen for the first time. In part the poem said,

> What I loved in my old life
> I haven't forgotten
> It lives in my spine
> Marianne and the child
> The days of kindness
> It rises in my spine
> And it manifests as tears
> I pray that a loving memory
> exists for them too
> the precious ones I overthrew
> for an education in the world.

Leonard Cohen, I believe, is a man who made the compromises necessary to exist in the world he chose and who created a shield — a very marketable shield, but still a shield — to keep his soul alive for his writing. In 1993, Cohen told the *Ottawa Citizen*'s Jay Stone that from the mid-1970s to the mid-1980s he felt he was becoming "a green grocer of despair." This seemed to me to be tremendously sad and, as I parted company with him that day, I asked him the simplest question of all.

"Are you a happy guy?"

"Sometimes. Sometimes."

"Most of the time?"

"I don't know," he sighed. "It's like that old joke. I had a job running an elevator many years ago in New York City and about five or ten times a day people would make the same joke, how's business? Up and down. That's about it."

I reminded him of another scene in Donald Britain's documentary in which Pierre Berton demanded to know how Cohen could claim to be a poet and not be bothered by the things that were going on in the world around him. As he looked back over his life, did he see things that bothered him now?

"I remember having a conversation with Nico, who was one of Andy Warhol's superstars, a beautiful and very talented woman. We were talking about Joan of Arc and I asked her, 'do you think Joan of Arc fell in love with anybody?' And Nico said, 'I think she fell in love with everybody.'" He smiled. "I think if Pierre Berton asked me the question now, I'd say I'm bothered by everything."

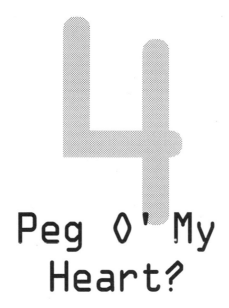

Peg O' My Heart?

Here's a confession: I'm not much of a fan of Margaret Atwood's writing. There are plenty of other authors and poets whose work I find more interesting and more moving. I thought *The Edible Woman* was clever, I thought *Life Before Man* was boring, and I thought *The Handmaid's Tale* had been done before and had a weak ending, but then, I'm a guy. I tried, Lord how I tried, to get through *The Robber Bride*. In fact, every once in awhile, I pick it up and try again. Not being able to enjoy it makes me feel somehow un-Canadian.

Having said all of this doesn't mean I don't like her, though. I've interviewed her at least three times and I think she's, well, cool. Besides I also know my opinion, or anybody else's for that matter, would mean less to her than the annoying buzz of a house fly.

Margaret Atwood is a rarity in Canadian literature; she is probably the most easily recognizable writer the country has ever produced. Even people who have never picked up a book, let alone a Canadian book, would likely know who she is by name, if not by sight.

Atwood is short and curly-haired and seems surrounded with a remarkably vivacious energy. It's difficult not to be immediately struck by her eyes, which are intense and lively and always seem to be taking part in some kind of joke to which only she is privy. In fact, that's one of the more disconcerting things about interviewing her; her eyes seldom leave yours, she is always aware of every remark made to her — even the throwaway ones — and she is always cracking jokes, yet you're left with the feeling after it's all over that the real joke was on you. It's easy to see why she bugs the hell out of so many people.

My first interview with Atwood happened in the fall of 1988 after the publication of her novel *Cat's Eye*. She had come to Ottawa to receive the Order of Canada and her publishers thought they might get in a bit of public relations at the same time.

The book showed up about two days before Atwood was scheduled to arrive at the studios, leaving me virtually no time to read it. Something told me I should admit this to her right away instead of trying to bluff. It's a good thing I did because by the time she left the studio, I was convinced she could have ripped my lungs out and served them up to me with a side of fries.

This was one of the few times I used a cheap trick to ingratiate myself to an author. The novel's title, *Cat's Eye*, was a reference to a type of marble used by children, and in the book the narrator's brother kept his in a Crown Royal bag. Like every other Canadian youngster, I too had played marbles and had kept them in the traditional Seagram's Crown Royal bag, a purple flannel sack with a yellow drawstring. I found one that my wife and I used for holding Scrabble letters, filled it with my daughter's marble collection, and brought it into the studio when Atwood arrived, keeping it out of sight under the edge of the table.

I began the interview with my admission about only being able to read part of the book, then brought the bag of marbles out. Atwood laughed, poured the marbles — which I told her I thought should properly be called "alleys" — out onto the table and asked, "Where did you get these?" Then with a twinkle in her eye, "These are — pardon me — these are awfully small."

We talked about the hierarchy of marbles, from waterbabies to cat's eyes to puries; we talked about the ways the game was played in different parts of the country; and then, never forgetful of why she was there, she steered the conversation back to the book. I commented that many critics had called *Cat's Eye* autobiographical. Her response gave me the first glimpse of the toughness just under her effervescent surface.

"If I want to call it an autobiography, I'm going to write that on the front," she stated flatly. "It's a novel. Now obviously the raw material is stuff that you pick up from your own experience and many another place, but it's a novel."

She had used the public school and the high school in her own life, she said, as the models for the schools in the book, but her own experiences were much different, perhaps even weirder, than what takes place in the story. Our conversation drifted to the cruelty of children to one another, and then she startled me by maintaining that little girls are much meaner to each other than little boys.

"The procedures are very different," she explained. "Little boys are very out on the table, they're very open. If they want to be mean to another little boy, a lot of it is physical — none of it is concealed under the guise of 'you're my best friend but there's something you need to know.' It's very clear what's going on.

"But little girls are much more, shall we say, byzantine about it. So instead of it being 'these guys are my friends and those guys are my enemies,' it's 'these people are my friends, but today they're all going off in the corner and not talking to me for some reason,' that kind of thing. Talk to anybody who has been a little girl, or a father or mother who has little girls, and they'll tell you that this type of behaviour occurs at the same time that little boys are off playing with one another and not paying much attention to little girls — except to shoot spitballs at them and that sort of thing."

The effects of this, Atwood claimed, were the establishment

very early in life of the male tendency to hide emotions and create pecking orders.

"I was a camp counsellor — you'll find this hilariously funny — at a coeducational summer camp and I had a cabin full of eight-year-old little boys. Why was it girl counsellors?" (Nothing makes an interviewer more insecure than the interviewee asking her own questions to herself, a commonplace Atwood practice I was to discover.) "Because they had had a male counsellor the summer before and one of these eight-year-old boys had gone the entire summer without having a bowel movement. Nobody had noticed."

"Good Lord," I murmured.

"So they thought that women were more conscious of these sorts of things," she added.

"More conscious of bodily functions, or more conscious of the kid in the corner who's about to explode?"

Atwood laughed. "They figured women would at least ask the question: 'how are you feeling today, dear?' So we were two female counsellors in this cabin of little boys, and it was very interesting to watch the pecking order because the top guy was really a nice guy. He was the biggest, he was the best at baseball, and he had the best selection of baseball cards, but he wasn't a tyrant. He was just somebody the other kids naturally looked up to. And that descended from there, and there was one little kid at the very bottom. But Neil, the top guy, was a bed-wetter and by the end of the summer every single kid in that cabin wet his bed at night, including the kid at the bottom of the pecking order who announced with great glee one morning that he had done this. So the thing that you would ordinarily get picked on for, because it was Neil doing it, everybody wanted to do it. By the end of the summer we had to wash the sheets every morning."

"Good thing it wasn't the kid with the bowel movement problem at the top of the pecking order," I mused.

I was feeling brave enough to shift the topic to something that had been receiving some public attention that season. In his memoirs, called *The Best Seat in the House*, Robert Fulford had included a passage about Atwood.

"And isn't it a winner too?" she commented dryly.

Fulford had suggested that Atwood took great pleasure in denying she wanted any public focus on her when, Fulford maintained, she really liked it.

"First of all, he starts off that axiom by misinterpreting something that I've said, which is not that I didn't want to be famous, but that I didn't expect to be famous," she complained. "Anybody knowing what it was like in Canada in the fifties and early sixties will realize that that was a totally legitimate lack of expectation. There weren't any famous writers when I was starting to be a writer. One happened along a little later — it was Irving Layton — but when I began, I didn't know there were any living Canadian writers. The only writers I knew were dead English people.

"So, he took that and misinterpreted it and then slammed me for some kind of hidden motive. Well, I think the most wonderful thing he said was that it was obvious that I was lusting for fame because I was chairman of The Writers' Union of Canada. And I'd like to give this sentiment wide publicity because then we wouldn't have so much trouble dragging people kicking and screaming into this unpaid, gruelling job. I did that in about 1978 when I was not lacking in fame, but I think it's a wonderful prescription for how to become famous, and now that he's written a book, we'll get him to be chairman and he can be famous."

She wasn't through yet. "There are some other quite wonderful things in there," she continued, obviously relishing the idea of sticking it to Fulford. "He did do an interview with me in which he did act rather intimidated, but was that my fault?" By now she was laughing again. "He said, 'I'm not envious of Margaret Atwood' after having detailed all these other people who were envious.

"An even more wonderful thing that I just love is that he said that feminism has been such a raging success. He tried to get me to do a piece once and the thesis of the piece was going to be, 'now that feminism is such a raging success we can all kind of forget about it and concentrate instead on the men who have been wounded by it.' I said, 'just a second, Bob, where do you get it that feminism is this raging success?' and he said 'I know all these famous women who appear so successful,' and I asked 'who?' and he said, 'Barbara Frum, Anna Porter, you, Rosalie Abella.' I said, 'name twenty others, and what about the fact that single mothers are now the fastest growing group below the poverty line? So I don't think I can do the piece.' So he did it himself."

With Robert Fulford's hide securely nailed to the wall, Atwood wrapped up the interview and said her goodbyes. I felt lucky to have gotten through the encounter unscathed — many other interviewers weren't as fortunate.

I didn't meet Atwood again until the fall of 1992. That meeting was to talk to her about her collection of prose and poetry, *Good Bones*, a small book put out by Coach House Press.

She bustled into the Toronto hotel room that had been set aside for the interview, bright and smiling. I began by telling her that many of the short pieces in *Good Bones* reminded me of Woody Allen — before the fall. That sent her into a whole recollection about Allen's best writing in *The New Yorker*, including a favourite piece of mine called "The Whore of Mensa."

"I know that Woody Allen is a bad person now and we're not supposed to like him," she said, "but that doesn't alter the fact that his early written stuff is brilliant."

This time it was my turn to bring the talk back to the book in question. I asked her if she found short works more appealing to write than an entire novel.

"Unless you're a James Joyce writing *Finnegan's Wake*, you could not write a novel-length manuscript that has this kind of condensation of language in it. It would just be too exhausting to read. He did do *Finnegan's Wake* — have you finished it?" she asked me suddenly, smiling wickedly.

Damn, I thought, *she's doing it again.* I tried the quick, witty comeback. "No, that and *Moby Dick,* speaking of Woody Allen."

"Well, *Moby Dick* I did finish because it's got a plot and also I read it when I was twelve and it had great pictures, so I was looking at the pictures." There was no beating this woman; I was saved from continuing as the unarmed man in a battle of wits only by Atwood's quickly shifting attention span. She was reminded of something else and she changed subjects instantly.

"I did a nice picture for this book, on the front," she said, picking up my copy of *Good Bones* and pointing to the collage on the cover. "I made it out of my daughter's used fashion magazines. I cut out all those little mouths and I cut out all those little eyes with my nail scissors and I stuck them on with my glue stick. Why did I do that?" she asked, once again supplying the question she apparently thought I hadn't been quick enough to ask myself. "It's a Coach House Press book; they would have had to pay somebody else." She smiled, "I did it for nothing."

Ignoring the very real possibility that I could replace Robert Fulford in Atwood's pantheon of idiotic men, I decided to broach the subject of her treatment of the male species in *Good Bones.*

"I'm pretty evenhanded," she smirked, staring straight at me defiantly.

"Oh no, how can you say that?" In for a penny, I thought.

"Come on," she countered, "I've got the Wicked Witch, the Evil Stepmother, and the Ugly Sister. I've got the Little Red Hen complaining. These are all female characters. It's true that I have a piece called 'Making a Man,' in which I give the recipe. But you have to see that as one of those fifties radio shows with the lady with the hat telling you how to cook things."

"But you do have lines in here," I protested, taking the book back from her and starting to flip through the pages, "I even marked a couple of them —"

"You probably don't mind the bad lines about women," she interrupted. "You probably think 'right on, hey, that's really accurate —'"

"No, I never suggested any such thing," I cut in.

"— and then when you come to the lines about men, you say 'that's not fair' — she put on a whining singsong voice — 'hey, this isn't fair . . . I know lots of guys who aren't . . . hey, I'm not like this . . . we aren't all like this.'"

I gave up and decided it was my turn to change topics. I asked her about the experience of having one of her novels — *The Handmaid's Tale* — turned into a film. What was the experience like, I wanted to know, and how did she feel about the result?

"Relieved," she answered. "I've known something about the movie business since about 1971, which was when I did my very first screenplay with Tony Richardson, who is, alas, no longer alive. I was adapting *Edible Woman* with him and that never came to anything for reasons that I won't go into here, which are, however, very bizarre. So I knew from the beginning what problems there are with films.

"Films are very, very visual," she said, being obvious and laughing at herself for it. "That's why we go to them, to see them. The most important thing about film is not the words — it's the pictures. You know this immediately when you try to remember a movie and what people actually said. And it's very hard to remember what came out of their mouths, but you can remember what they did. Also movies are shorter and they also lock you in. You go in, you sit in a movie, and it's like sitting in an airplane: you're in that movie and you have to go in the direction that the movie is going. And when it's over, it's over. You can't turn back the pages, you can't start at the back and go forward. You are really being dictated to by that film. You also can't easily jump time, unless you're Mel Brooks. You can't say, 'okay, it's two thousand years later.' You also can't do similes and metaphors. You can't say 'Christ is a lion' unless you wish to make a very surreal movie in which you actually see Christ turning into a lion. But you can't use language in the way that writers use language all the time. You're very limited to the visual, to the evident, to the what you can see."

Atwood was in full flight now, not looking at me but staring out of the hotel room window at the boats on Lake Ontario.

"So I knew what to expect," she went on, returning to the filming of *A Handmaid's Tale*. "I knew they would have to leave things out. They did. I knew that they wouldn't be able to do a lot of flashbacks. They didn't. I knew they wouldn't be able to do that bit at the end where we go forward two hundred and fifty years. They tried. They tried all kinds of ways of doing it, but it just wouldn't have worked. And I knew that they would have to put more action in because a lot of the story is somebody sitting in a chair, thinking and breathing and being very 'inner.' Unless you use voice-over and are Ingmar Bergman, there's just no way you can do that.

"So I knew all of those things and, within its parameters, it's very good. It's very well acted, it goes forward, it's certainly very gripping, and it upsets people a lot. But it's not the same as the book."

I asked her if she would ever consider going through the experience again. She pointed out that it was Harold Pinter, not her, who had written the screenplay.

"I have done screenplays. It's fun, but for a writer it's sort of like summer camp for grown-ups. You're with a bunch of people, you're locked into a situation with them, and if you get on, it's lots of fun and you have a good time, and if you don't get on, it can be hell. But the other thing about movies is that they involve such a huge amount of money up front. Huge, enormous amounts of money are involved in making movies and that limits your freedom a lot. You have much more freedom as a writer sitting there with just your page. You can put anything on that page that you want to. Then it's another thing when that page goes out to meet the reader, that's another condition. But when you're in the room with that page, it's just you. Nobody is saying, 'You can't do that! I put five million dollars into this! You can't do that! I've got control of this picture!'"

Since four years had gone by since my last interview with Atwood, and since we were already talking about entertainment, I decided it might be interesting to raise, once again, the concept of writer as celebrity. I asked her why she thought it was that so many writers seemed to be upset over the attention paid to them.

"It's because they've seen what's happened to certain others," she replied. "Others who have believed their own billboards and have essentially turned into two-dimensional cardboard statues of themselves."

I asked if she worried about the attention paid to her. Robert Fulford's ears must have been ringing.

"It doesn't really get paid to me," she explained, grinning. "It gets paid to my uncontrollable twin. All the pictures you see in the paper are of that person."

"The Evil Twin?" I almost giggled.

"She's not evil — she's just not under my control. I'm not accountable for what happens to that person. She's out there being in the papers and I'm back in my room with my page."

The mischievous twinkle was back in her eye as she leaned forward in her chair. "So, you know, don't blame me."

5

Wrestling with John Irving

American author John Irving reached that rarified plateau of writer/celebrity in the 1980s with his novel *The World According to Garp*. Not only did the book do well on the bestseller charts, but it was also turned into a modestly successful Hollywood movie starring Robin Williams.

Not long after, Irving married a Canadian and began splitting his time between Canada and his New England home. That Canadian connection appeared strongly in his novel *A Prayer for Owen Meany*, which not only had Canadian locales, but also used a literary homage to Robertson Davies's The Deptford Trilogy as a key incident in its plot.

I had read *The World According to Garp* twice and enjoyed it very much. I also liked the movie treatment of it (Irving made a cameo appearance as a wrestling referee). I was disappointed in his next novel, *The Hotel New Hampshire*, which seemed too self-conscious in its casual violence. The film version of that novel, starring Jodie Foster, was a box-office failure.

So I was interested to see on which side of the line *Owen Meany* would fall. I was even more intrigued when I received an audio excerpt from the novel, read by Irving, in which he re-created the almost indescribable high-pitched voice of his diminutive protagonist. I eagerly bought the book. I found that I didn't like it as much as *Garp*, but found it far better than *Hotel New Hampshire*.

When John Irving came into the studio to talk about his writing, he fairly vibrated with good health. Damn, I thought, this guy is a few years older than me and he looks like he could wrestle alligators without breaking a sweat. He was short and stocky, movie-star handsome, and had a strong, clean-shaven jaw, just the right amount of grey streaking his dark hair, piercing, intelligent eyes, and a fierce intensity when speaking. I found him amiable and generous with his time, more than willing to sit and answer my questions for as long as I felt like asking them.

Common themes of predestination, random and unexpected violence, and unhappy conclusions run through Irving's novels. I had chosen three quotes from *Owen Meany* that I thought illustrated these themes. The first was: "Every study of the gods, of everyone's gods, is a revelation of vengeance towards the innocent"; the second was: "Coincidence was a stupid, shallow refuge sought by stupid, shallow people who are unable to accept the fact that their lives are shaped by a terrifying and awesome design"; and the final quote was: "We are a civilization careening towards a succession of anticlimaxes, towards an infinity of unsatisfying and disagreeable endings."

"If you put those three quotes together," I began, "would it be fair to say that they would constitute the thrust of the themes you're trying to deal with in this book?"

Irving threw his head back and laughed loudly, showing perfect white teeth. "I would say that's very accurate," he replied. "It's a coming-together of a very old-fashioned, Thomas Hardy sense of fate, or a cruel destiny, with an almost Calvinistic sense of predestination. It's a religious novel only in the sense that the man telling the story has been converted by a miracle he must bear witness to. And the miracle is, compared to the Christian miracle and the New Testament as a whole, very small and considerably grotesque. It's a contemporary version of that story.

As witness to this miracle, the man who has seen it and survived the life of his friend is somewhat of a wreck. It always occurred to me in thinking of a miracle . . . that if I were a witness to something that could make a believer out of me, it would also destroy me in the process."

If the themes in *Garp* included terrifying designs and disagreeable endings mounted on a framework of political incorrectness (like taking feminism to a frightening extreme), *Owen Meany*'s themes of violence were played out against a background of religion. A key plot element involved a childish hoax that results in an unshakeable faith on the part of its victim, an irony of belief that Irving said came out of his own religious feelings as a child.

"It's an irony to me," he said, "when I think of the countless people who are comforted — as a child I certainly was — by that great Christian story, the story of the New Testament. People who accept on faith that miracle. It interests me and, more than interests, amuses me to imagine how much of that miracle would we believe today if there were even a partial second coming — even a Christ who asked us to believe an eighth as much as that first Christ demanded our attention to believe. My suspicion is we would mock and ridicule that character and treat him far more badly than we treated the first messenger."

Irving, in his novels, creates unshakeable faith in his characters through violent acts rather than words. *The World According to Garp* uses brutality to propel the story along and *A Prayer for Owen Meany* uses violence as the central spine of the story. I asked Irving what it was in him that made him see the universe as such a savage place.

"I think that the lives of all of us are extremely precarious and fragile," he explained. "We are dependent so often on a fate or accident that we cannot control . . . can we really not help fearing any number of calamities that, on the front page of the paper every day, appear inevitable? We live in a time of disaster, if for no other reason than that the coverage of disaster is all around us in a way that it never was in the 1940s. If there is a disaster any-where, we know of it. And I think we spend much of our lives projecting ourselves into this climate of disaster.

"If you look at the contemporary history of the United States alone, just imagine how much of it has been predetermined by the assassination of both Kennedys. Without those assassinations we are looking at the possibility of two terms in office of three Kennedy brothers in a row. Now that's twenty-four years of liberal, democratic presidents commencing in 1960. I think one can safe-ly say that the history of the U.S. was enormously changed by those two accidents."

The protagonist in *Owen Meany* is John Wheelwright, a man teaching at Bishop Strachan College in Toronto, looking back over his past, reading the *Globe and Mail* and the *New York Times*, and railing about the condition of his native land, the United States. Since Irving was spending much of his time in Toronto, it was natural to inquire if the feelings John Wheelwright had about the States as an exile were also the feelings of John Irving.

"I've had the advantage of living outside of the United States a number of times," he told me. "Not only since I married a Canadian, but I lived eight years in Austria prior to that, and I spent some time in England and in Greece. One of the opinions I share with Wheelwright is that Americans would learn to see themselves far better if they spent more time out of their own country and acquainted themselves just the smallest amount with how they are perceived by the rest of the world. That is an educa-tion. I think I largely had that education before I started living here.

"My own political anger is a lot more tempered than John Wheelwright's. The sadness of Wheelwright is that he is one of those expatriates for whom the expatriation has failed. He only thinks he's a Canadian; he is a citizen — he has given up his country — but the virulency of his anti-Americanism, in a way, makes him a more attached American than half of those indifferent citizens still living back home. He's like a dog who needs to dig up the same bone. His anger, his loathing of the U.S., is really datable to 1968 when he came here, and he has a kind of knee-jerk political reaction to every headline that comes across the border and provokes him and taunts him. My point about all of that is that there are countless Johnny Wheelwrights who were victims of those Vietnam years and whose political cynicism can be dated directly to that time, and they're not all living in Toronto or Stockholm. I know a lot of Johnny Wheelwrights who are living in Massachusetts and Vermont."

In *Owen Meany* Irving places Robertson Davies's name, along with Thomas Hardy and others, among a list of important authors. The opening chapter of the book describes an event that bears a striking resemblance to Davies's fateful snowball in The Deptford Trilogy.

"This book has many literary tips of the hat, not only to the New Testament," he explained. "Owen Meany's story is a parody of a small piece of the New Testament, plain and simple. Owen Meany himself has more than the first initials in common with Oskar Matzerath, the little fellow in *The Tin Drum*, that notion of a character who doesn't grow and whose smallness is itself a kind of symbol for a moral indignation at his times. I read that Günter Grass novel when I was in university, and there's probably no book that caught me at a time when I was more easily influenced by a book than that one.

"And my baseball, the baseball that Owen Meany hits that kills his best friend's mother, my baseball is both a piece of homage and a mischievous parody of Rob Davies's snowball, to be sure.

"These are little things that you hope that readers of books in common sort of recognize and share. If they're not seen, if no one picks them up, then there's no harm done. But I get the pleasure of it and it's not so much in the nature of an inside joke in that nothing is lost if you don't pick up on it."

He began laughing, "But in *The World According to Garp*, the whole history of Garp's father is very consciously modelled on that terrible victim in Joe Heller's *Catch-22*, yet I read almost nothing about that and the first person who ever said anything about it to me — who said, 'hey, I got that' — was Joe Heller."

6

With a
Little Help
from
My Friends

The musicians in this chapter all have one thing in common: they survived. Some of them made it through the shifting sands of public taste by the sheer force of their talent, and some survived the seemingly inevitable self-destruction of the rock music business by the sheer force of their will. I went out of my way to interview each one of them.

❏

Joe Cocker came to Ottawa on a bill that included Michelle Shocked, the Neville Brothers, and Bob Dylan.

It was late in the evening by the time Cocker finished his performance, and I was hanging out behind the large, specially erected stage in the middle of a football field going over notes on his career in anticipation of a scheduled interview. He and his band and backup singers came sweating and whooping down the stairs in back of the platform, high-fiving each other as they crossed the twenty yards of field to the locker rooms that served as dressing rooms.

Twenty minutes later, a freshly showered Cocker emerged and I immediately steered him in the direction of the mobile studio downfield. As we walked along, chatting about the concert, a couple of people with backstage passes cut in to get autographs and take pictures. As we reached the mobile, out of the corner of my eye I saw two people running towards us, one of them shouting Cocker's name. Damn, I thought, another delay. The guy doing the yelling said, "Joe, Bob just wanted to say hi," and he turned and left.

There, standing in long-collared white shirt with billowy sleeves, black leather vest, and jeans tucked into motorcycle boots, was Bob Dylan. I won't say my heart stopped, because that would be unseemly. I will say I caught my breath and held it for what could easily have been ten minutes.

"Sorry I missed you in Naples," Dylan croaked, and they carried on an inane conversation while the announcer out front introduced Dylan and the crowd began to roar.

For those who have the same cultural connection to Bob Dylan that I have had over three decades, a couple of impressions might be interesting: he reeked of alcohol but didn't appear drunk so maybe, just maybe, it was some kind of obscure aftershave; he was taller than I expected, but it could have been the biker boots; and his skin looked like very dry, very fragile parchment paper about to disintegrate, as if a simple touch would turn him to dust. He was not a healthy-looking individual.

"Well, gotta go," Dylan said finally and, hiking his electric guitar strap around his neck, he ran off in the direction of the stage.

Cocker and I resumed our walk to the nearby mobile. "That was Bob Dylan," I said to him. I was, ahem, a bit flustered.

"Yes," he replied, eyeing me sideways, "it was."

We climbed the three tight steps into the mobile and squeezed into seats at a small table wired with microphones that were recording the conversation over a microwave link back to the studio.

For a man who had just come off of a strenuous hour-long holler, Joe Cocker looked remarkably relaxed, even placid. There was none of that hyperactive twitchiness that John Belushi had captured so perfectly nearly two decades earlier. He was greying where he wasn't balding and had a very lived-in face. Only when he spoke did that naturally gravelly voice betray a touch of strain; other than that, he could just as easily have come in from a few holes of golf.

One of the things I have always admired about Cocker is his ability to choose songs to record with an unerring sense of the appropriate. The only other example of that almost consistent talent seemed to be Rod Stewart, bad hair notwithstanding.

Cocker said he used no particular method for selecting material, often just going with what his friends and sidemen suggested. He told me, for instance, that he was initially reluctant to cover the Beatles song "You've Got To Hide Your Love Away" because it was in three-four time and his first major hit, another Beatles tune "With a Little Help from My Friends," was also in three-four. He gently suggested to me that he did "interpretations" not "covers," and arrangements for them often came after ten or twelve takes in the studio with the musicians "live on the floor."

Cocker talked about his love of Ray Charles's vocal style — his biggest obvious influence — and his admiration for the singing of Marvin Gaye and Donny Hathaway. "Strangely, a lot of the people I like are dead," he commented dryly.

Cocker himself had been a prime candidate for the roll call of dead rock musicians. Stories abound of his years of crazed substance abuse and the massive amounts of alcohol that often left him incapable of even standing up on stage. One story suggested Jane Fonda had helped him through this period of his life by giving him a place to stay on her California ranch.

He laughed. "Only indirectly," he said. "It was actually my wife, Pam, who I met at Jane Fonda's ranch — well, I was living in L.A. and I was pretty messed up at the time and I wanted to get out of the city. I was grateful to Jane for renting me this house on her ranch, because she had her doubts about letting me live there. But then I found out later it was my wife who swung the vote to get me up there."

How messed up was "pretty messed up"?

"In a period from about 1975 to about '77 I must admit that I'd go on stage and I'd barely remember the tours. It was a pretty sad place to be in, you know. But I think what pulled me out was Germany — it was always a pretty stable place for me to play in, even when things weren't going well in the States. It was amazing. I remember doing a show one night when I thought I was really awful and yet the crowd was still super to me. It sort of twigged something inside of me. I thought, 'hey, Joe, if the kids are going to be that good, you owe them something a bit better to give back.' And I slowly started coming out of it and making the music the focus and not the drugs."

We talked for a few minutes about his distinctive, raspy voice and how he learned over the years to sing from the solar plexus to keep from putting too much strain on his vocal chords.

Finally, I thought I would try to pry a confession out of him. I wanted to get this hard-rocking, booze-swilling, gravel-throated, chain-smoking, soulful blues singer to admit that his famous duet with Jennifer Warnes, "Up Where We Belong" from the Richard Gere/Debra Winger film *An Officer and a Gentleman*, was the abomination I had always thought it was. I knew that, even now, Cocker sometimes included this tune written by the otherwise gifted Canadian Buffy St. Marie in his concerts as a duet with his longtime backup singer Maxine Sharpe. I tried to gently ease into the subject.

"That was the most successful song you've ever done in financial terms, isn't it?" I asked.

"Well, it was number one in the States, yeah," he replied.

"Now holding that song up against all of the other things you do," I ventured, "I know I think, 'well, I guess it's just something he's got to do to pay the rent.' Do you feel that way about it?"

He was cautious. "Well, I really didn't like the song when I first heard it," he admitted. "It took me a lot of being talked into, to do it. But, actually, I'm going to be doing a few concerts with

Jennifer in Europe and it will be interesting to see how the song goes now."

"But do you like it now?" I pressed.

"Yeah ... well ... yeah ... I still ... no, well," he started laughing, ". . . I like Maxine's treatment of it."

❏

Bonnie Raitt was sounding a bit exasperated and it was making me nervous. We were sitting backstage at the Mariposa Folk Festival in the early summer of 1988 after she had just finished a well-received set of tunes in front of an enthusiastic audience. She was sitting on a couch in her dressing room, sipping on soda water, and trying to answer my questions, but I was asking about parts of her career that made her irritable.

This didn't make me feel very good either because I was a huge admirer of Raitt's music and had been for many years. My slight apprehension over talking to her had led me to make a stupid mistake in my first question and it was almost all downhill from there. I knew she had been influenced greatly by "Sippie" Wallace, the blues singer from the twenties. Raitt had even arranged to have Wallace brought out of retirement. I inadvertently referred to the late singer as "Slippie." It wasn't until Raitt bore down on the correct name as she gazed coolly at me through half-closed eyes that I realized my mistake. I almost gulped out loud.

It took Bonnie Raitt nearly twenty years in the music business to make it big, but when I spoke with her she was still about six or seven months away from the 1989 release of her multiplatinum, Grammy-winning album *Nick of Time*. She had just been dropped by Warner Brothers, and had been picked up by Capitol, but the experience had made her bitter and she was having trouble hiding it.

Bonnie Raitt was born in California, the daughter of tenor John Raitt, who had gained fame in such films as *The Pajama Game* and

Broadway plays like *Carousel.* Her Quaker parents sent her to a Quaker-run summer camp in the Adirondack Mountains in New England, where as a teenager she learned about social issues from the college-age counsellors. She also heard old blues players like Odetta and Mississippi John Hurt and found their music an appealing antidote to the beach-boy scene in her home state. When it came time to go to university, she chose Radcliffe College, not for its programs but because it was close to Cambridge, Massachusetts, and the burgeoning folk music scene at a coffee-house called Club 47. There she met the likes of Son House and Buddy Guy and Fred McDowell. She started playing the New England coffee houses, dropped out of school, and began a career that would take her on a roller-coaster ride of blues, booze, career frustration, and, finally, success beyond her wildest expectations.

Raitt had signed onto the full blues-singer package, complete with overindulgence in all the usual vices. Her drinking and partying were notorious and added to the appeal of her raw bottleneck guitar and raspy voice. But by that summer of 1988, she had given it all up.

"The reason I quit getting loaded," she told me, "was because I'm thirty-eight and it wasn't looking good on me and it didn't feel good on me. Hangovers are no fun when you're thirty-five, let alone thirty-eight, and for those of us that like to party a lot — I mean, I never did it before my shows, but I did it a fair amount afterwards — after awhile it just got kind of old. I don't recommend excess for anybody at anytime, but twenty years down the road it's going to wear anybody out. Your only free time is at night because the rest of the day you spend getting to where you're going to play. So you spend five or six hours in the bus and most of the time you're asleep because nobody can stay awake — I don't care how good the movie is — on the bus. After awhile, months and months on the road, you end up with not enough exercise and not enough good food, and late at night you're not eating popcorn and drinking milk, let's face it."

I asked why the change happened so far down the road for her.

"It can happen at any age," she answered. "I look around at people who are my age, who are the ones I'm in touch with, and I think that the time to re-evaluate your life can happen at any point. I know lots of people who are in their twenties who are not doing blow anymore, and, thank God, we saved them another ten years of forgetting what they said."

Despite those years of excess, Raitt never stopped putting out her own brand of rootsy, funky rhythm and blues. Yet a loyal, steady following did not give her any kind of access to radio air-play, at least the kind of airplay that could translate into sales and success. She had had plenty of time to think about the reasons why.

"There's just not enough room for ethnic music," she said. "It's big corporate radio. They want to make as much money as they can, then sign another act that can make as much money as the one last week. And if you're not interested in selling millions of records — which I don't really care about, I just want to make music and have my fans be able to buy it and listen to it on the radio — you're out of luck these days."

Her bitterness with Warner Brothers, her former label, came to the surface when I asked why certain of her records, which I thought had marketability, never seemed to go anywhere.

"Warner Brothers decided not to promote my records after I re-signed with them." Her anger was tangible. "They were expecting me to be Linda Ronstadt or something and when I didn't pan out to be that, they just moved on to someone else who was going to sell more records, frankly. At that point, there was punk and new wave — there were a lot of reasons why I wasn't played. My older fans didn't want to hear me do rock 'n' roll, and my newer fans didn't think I was hard-edged enough. I'm kind of in that musical no-man's-land. There's nothing wrong with what I do, it's just that the radio stations that would normally play me are not as plentiful. To the purists who want to hear just the folk music, I'm too commercial and to the ones who want to hear me sound more like Toto, I'm too folky. It's just one of those dilemmas. That's why I'm performing without a band most of the time."

That dilemma was soon to evaporate almost overnight. Raitt gave me some indications of the things her new record label, Capitol, was willing to let her do on the soon-to-be-released *Nick of Time* album.

"Capitol agrees that we can make a record that will be not necessarily tremendously expensive to make and will reflect the times — which includes people like Tracy Chapman and Suzanne Vega. So we can make a stripped-down, rootsy record and get radio airplay. I don't put all the blame on Warner Brothers. They have Madonna and Prince and Van Halen and Paul Simon; they don't really have room to push somebody who's only going to sell three hundred thousand copies. But as long as you can keep your expenses down, you can make money in this business and have records. Sometimes you just need to switch — like a bad marriage, you got to move and get to something more positive. Capitol has Joe Cocker and Robert Palmer and Richard Thompson, and those are all people with whom I identify musically and age-wise and we'll see if we can just market to a different target audience."

It was here that I managed to make myself the focus of her irritability: I asked her if Capitol was pressuring her to make a record with wider audience appeal.

"Well, I'd have to be pretty stupid not to do that myself," she shot back. "Everybody, when they put out a record, thinks they've got a song on it that everybody wants to hear. I didn't put horns and strings on my songs on my other albums just because Warner Brothers tied me to a chair and said I had to be commercial. I put them on because I think it sounds good. I'm not going to change my style to fit something that's not me just to get airplay. What I do have to do is pay attention to the fact that out of ten songs on an album, there should be at least one or two that should probably get airplay, otherwise no record company is going to put it out."

She paused, considering her anger, then suddenly laughed. My relief was instantaneous. "I can press them myself in my house. If you want to be played on radio you've got to make music that sounds like something somewhat similar to what people want to hear. A good song is a good song in any period of time. There's not really any rules."

When we finished and I had turned off the tape recorder, Bonnie Raitt smiled and said, "Whew. That was like a business seminar." I've always hoped she meant it as a compliment.

❐

He is called Dr. John the Night Tripper, with a bottle of gris gris in his hand. His real name is Malcolm (Mac) John Rebbenack and he is the embodiment of the soul of New Orleans.

Like the city of Montreal, New Orleans doesn't seem like part of the country it inhabits. It is a unique place, steeped in the customs, music, religions, and politics of a hundred different nationalities. Sprawling there in the heat at the mouth of the Mississippi River, New Orleans has been responsible for the creation of jazz and the birth of rock 'n' roll, all bubbling through with a music that combines voodoo from Haiti, obeah from Jamaica, any number of African rhythms, and the zydeco of the Cajuns and Creoles. It is a potent mix and Mac Rebbenack has been central to all of it for more than forty years.

Born in 1941 to a fashion-model mother and a record-store-owner father, Rebbenack spent his early years soaking up the sounds all around him. By his teens he was an accomplished musician, specializing in piano and playing with many of New Orleans's established performers, the "made" artists, including the legendary Professor Longhair. He put together AFO (All For One), a cooperative recording label for black musicians who were having trouble getting recorded elsewhere. By the mid-sixties he had migrated to Los Angeles where he was much in demand as a session musician and where he recorded with artists like Sam Cooke and Sonny and Cher.

In 1968 he released his first solo album, *Dr. John the Night Tripper*, and almost immediately became a cult figure with a psychedelic/gris gris/mardi gras/gumbo alter ego. His biggest commercial success came in 1973 with the album *In the Right Place*. For a few years during the eighties and early nineties, he went back to being just plain Mac Rebbenack, touring on his own and with musicians like the Neville Brothers and Ringo Starr. In 1992, he released the ultimate "N'Awlins" roots album, *Goin' Back to New Orleans*, followed in early 1994 with his funkiest Dr. John collection in years, *Television*.

I met Mac Rebbenack backstage one night in a club where he was playing. With the warm-up band doing its sound check behind us, we sat squashed knee-to-knee in his tiny dressing room. He was decked out in his trademark beret with a scraggly beard and a collection of arcane rings on most of his fingers. Although he is a thoroughly pleasant and unassuming man, I confess it took me a few minutes to be able to understand him. While the lyrics to the songs he sings are usually clear, that characteristic scratchy voice combined with his thick New Orleans accent makes normal conversation a bit tricky.

He told me his interest in music came early because of his father's line of work.

"My father used to stock these hotels on South Rampart Street with all these records, and he used to bring them home when they were used, so I'd get all these good old records from Memphis Minnie and Big Bill Broonzy and everybody from Hank Williams to Miles Davis to you-name-'em. That really got me started listening to records when I was about four or five years old. My pa used to ask me, way back then, what was my favourite record? And I had a list of them when I was like five years old, man. I liked 'Give Me That Old Time Religion' and 'Blueberry

Hill' and whatever. I had a whole list of songs that I was crazy about as a little bitty baby."

I was curious about his musical life in the mid-fifties when he was only in his early teens but was backing up some of the most serious musical heavyweights of the time.

"I had the only rock 'n' roll and rhythm 'n' blues band that could read music in New Orleans," he croaked. "So we backed all those shows that came through. Beside that, I had the only guys who could do the record dates — I had the open scene on most all of that stuff."

Rebbenack was also producing records around this period, despite his tender age, and one of them, "Mardi Gras in New Orleans," is still a hit every year at the carnival. The song was recorded by Roy Bird, known by his other handle "Professor Longhair." Fes, as he was called, died a very old man in the late seventies, but for decades his rolling, syncopated piano style formed the essence of the New Orleans sound. To Mac Rebbenack and his musician friends, Fes was a god.

"When I was coming up, everyone, from Hughie Smith, Allan Toussaint, Art Neville, every piano player around — even Fats Domino — had some Professor Longhair in him, and Fats was a made artist. Fes was the funk leader of New Orleans so everybody had to tip their hat to the guy who was so far ahead of the thing. He was also a guy who was an influence as a band leader. When I was working with Roy Brown at Lincoln Beach in New Orleans in the late fifties, when Longhair said do we want to go to work for him, we quit a six-night-a-week job to go to work one night a month for Professor Longhair. We didn't even give Roy Brown two weeks' notice. We left a six-night-a-week job to go maybe work once a month. You gotta look at that as something different. We're not known for being businessmen, that's for damn sure," he scratched out a raucous laugh.

"Tell me about AFO, then," I asked, wondering about his real business acumen.

"Well, it was at a time when the studio band was making a lot of hits for people and not getting no money for doing what all they did. AFO said, 'well, let's see if the musicians can make some money out of this deal' and started off with the first two records — 'She Put the Hurt on Me' by Prince LaLa and 'I Know' by Barbara George — and the first two records was instant hits. Now you'd think it would be a success story but, unfortunately, there was no businessmens in the AFO. You had guys who were great musicians but not great business guys. AFO got burnt for money left and right, and went under. I wound up going out to California, when the studio scene folded in New Orleans, and most of us guys went out to work for Sam Cooke out there."

The creation of the Dr. John persona was hugely successful for Rebbenack, but it was not without controversy. At the time stories were being written suggesting that he had ripped the idea off from his friend Prince LaLa. Rebbenack said it wasn't like that at all.

"Prince LaLa's brother was one of my guitar teachers — Papouse," he said. "And LaLa's family has always been very close friends of mine. There was pictures of him, and he — and his family — was into that whole scene for real and so there was a connection from the family turning me on to a lot of things I would use. But not just LaLa hisself, it was his whole family."

Yet the combination of voodoo trappings and the new psychedelia of the sixties seemed, in retrospect, like a cunning marketing move. Rebbenack surprised me by admitting that it was just a one-time idea he had and that originally it had been planned for somebody else, not for him.

"To be honest, I didn't think it was necessarily going to click," he confessed. "It was just a concept I had for one album I wanted to do. I wanted to do it originally with Ronnie Barron and his manager wouldn't let him do it and I got disgusted and just did it myself when I got a chance to do it. I just figured it would be a one-off deal and that would be the end of it. But it got caught up in the psychedelical craze and that was the weirdest thing of it, 'cause here we was trying to present a New Orleans gris gris, mardi gras–type show and we were being called everything but that. In a way, after awhile it didn't bug me anymore, but at first it threw me a lot of curves because we were doing one thing and being called a million other things. But as long as we were getting to do that stuff, the band was strong, then I didn't much care."

Rebbenack said the solo albums he recorded in the late eighties and early nineties have allowed him to get work almost constantly, touring by himself in between the tours with a band. Albums like *Dr. John Plays Hoagy Carmichael* and *In a Sentimental Mood* allowed him to toy with something he always thought could easily become his own future.

"I always looked at doing one of them kind of records that was like, okay, from here on it's just the Holiday Inn forever." He smiled. "You know, playing in the lounge all by myself? I got a kick out of doing it. But it opened up whole new areas of music for me . . . and that's what I'm basically looking for, because I like to play music, you know?"

❏

Interviewing Warren Zevon is like pulling teeth — through your ear. It's not that he's uncooperative in any traditional sense, foul-tempered, or irritable; it's just that he would much rather be doing anything else besides being asked questions. So he adopts a bemused, monosyllabic set of responses that is almost impossible to penetrate.

Zevon sat in the studio wearing round, steel-framed glasses, his hair pulled back in a ponytail, smirking at me through two days growth of beard. It was just after the release of his industrial/hi-tech album *Transverse City* — an album that vanished in the blink of an eye. I led the way musically into the interview by playing one of the few songs he had ever written that seemed to contain any vulnerability, a song called "Reconsider Me."

"Something from the romantic side," he sneered, as the song wound down. "A rare glimpse of the sensitive side of things."

"In fact, an extremely rare glimpse," I countered. "In *Transverse City* you seem to have the worst bad mood on imaginable."

"I dunno," he chuckled darkly, "I thought it was kind of a cheerful album, myself. I seem to be the only one who feels that way, though. Even my mother says this album's not funny."

Apparently most of the record-buying public agreed with Zevon's mother. The album contained forty minutes of music boiled down from what he told me was fourteen hundred hours of recorded material. It was being described as a *concept* album, a term Zevon said he was getting to dislike more and more as his *Millennial Paranoia* tour wore on. And the true depth of his cynicism was evident when I pressed him to characterize the record as something else.

"I was intrigued by the idea of, and some of the writers who were described as, cyberpunk. Which is sort of a meaningless term for some newer science fiction writers, and I had never read much science fiction previous to coming across this. So I decided, because it was also a glib answer to give in interviews before this came out, that I was going to do a cyberpunk album and it was going to be a little futuristic and it was kind of going to be a "life in 2010" album. And I think it ended up, after a track or two, being just about . . . a contemporary urban nightmare . . . ," he began to laugh as I started shaking my head at his words. "I've learned to speak entirely in those kind of blurbs — Los Angeles, present day, perhaps."

Zevon's career hit a peak in the mid-seventies with songs like "Werewolves of London," "Lawyers, Guns and Money," and "Excitable Boy" — songs that he claimed to still have a fondness for. But it wasn't until the early nineties that he came perilously close to commercial success again with his album, *Sentimental Hygiene*. The title track got plenty of radio play and the rock press was set to pounce on the songwriter with demands about the meaning of the phrase "sentimental hygiene." Zevon was ready for them.

"I had a whole set of evasive answers to that question and I can go down the list . . . ," he paused and smirked again. "It means love, doesn't it?"

I stared silently at him, smiling.

"Now you're disappointed. You want one of the evasive answers now?" he laughed. "Alright, let's try one of the exotic answers: Woman sends me a letter, says my four-year-old son says 'Mom, what does sentimental hygiene mean?' and I told him, 'it means keeping your feelings clean, and I keep my feelings so clean you can eat off them,' thank you, blah, blah, blah. That was a good answer," Zevon smirked. "Mine was hopelessly inadequate, so I'll just write the songs and not explain them, which is what I've been trying to do for twelve years."

"Does that bother you," I asked, "having to explain your songs to people?"

"Oh sure it's how I feel . . ."

"Would you be tempted to take the music end of it out, and just write?"

"On the contrary," he replied, seeming to be seriously considering a question for the first time in the interview, "I'd rather take the lyrics out altogether and just write music a lot of the time." He said he found composing and recording music for motion picture soundtracks the most "liberating and exhilarating" experience he had ever had. "I would be very happy to keep doing it in between writing songs, because I don't have any control over songwriting. I get an idea, always a lyrical idea, and I go to work and, depending on whether I have a deadline, I get the job done. So there is no reason why I can't write this the rest of the time. And, in fact, writing a song, as you have no doubt often heard, takes twenty minutes and a couple of years and another twenty minutes. Writing classical-type instrumental music takes . . . if I work for ten hours then I'll get ten minutes written. You work and you accomplish something."

❏

A record company ferret at one of Richard Thompson's former labels once said the press loved Thompson but radio stations wouldn't play him. When I read him the quote, the gangly, mild-mannered guitarist and songwriter laughed and said, "You can think that . . . but you're never supposed to say it."

Richard Thompson has long enjoyed a small (in record-industry terms) but loyal following ever since he appeared on the scene as a member of the 1960s British band Fairport Convention. He has approached the edges of commercial success several times as a solo artist, but has always veered away in time to keep his reputation intact. This image of a talented, uncompromising, laid-back rebel has made him a favourite of critics and other musicians. In 1994 (the year of the tribute album), a homage to Thompson's work, called *Beat the Retreat*, was released, featuring covers of his songs by the likes of Bonnie Raitt, Eric Clapton, R.E.M., and David Byrne.

Back in the mid-sixties when the British music scene was overflowing with the psychedelia of early Pink Floyd and the blues-edged rock of the Rolling Stones, Fairport Convention was working the same folk idiom as other English groups like The Incredible String Band and Pentangle. "When we were finding Joni Mitchell songs it was before she'd ever made a record," Thompson told me, as he sat idly playing his guitar in my studio. "It was about 1966 or something and, through a friend of a friend, we got demo tapes — we got demos of the basement tapes, of Dylan, before anybody else got hold of them. And, at that time, this singer/songwriter, lyric-orientated music wasn't that popular. Certainly in Britain it was almost unknown, and one of the reasons we wanted to do it was because we wanted to be different and we didn't want to play white soul music or white blues, which was the *lingua franca* at the time in Britain."

Being different didn't do any harm to the band because, under the banner of psychedelia, "everybody had a record contract who could open their mouths — it was quite extraordinary — including ourselves."

By 1971, Richard Thompson had begun feeling the urges that overcome most genuinely talented people when the constraints of band life get too tight. He struck out on his own with a solo album called *Henry, the Human Fly*. "Indeed," he intoned, when reminded of the effort. "What a record! It's a very quirky record — I must be an eccentric person to have made a record like this. Rumour has it that it was Warner Brothers's lowest-ever-selling record in the States. I'm very proud of that, obviously," he smiled, admitting that while he listened to his old material every few years for reference purposes, there were some stiffs that he still avoided.

It wasn't until 1982, and the release of *Shoot Out the Lights*, that Richard Thompson came "hideously" close to commercial success and finally achieved a sense of satisfaction with his own work. "I've been reasonably happy with the last few albums (since *Shoot Out the Lights*), or have felt there has been some consistency . . . I guess I'd better carry on . . . this is okay as a job," he smiled. "Mother was wrong."

A large part of Richard Thompson's appeal is the sense of maturity and solidity he brings to his work. He writes about adult themes set in a musical form that is usually associated with adolescent longings and frustrations, teenage angst, and he sees no contradiction in this. "I think rock 'n' roll is now broad enough and multigenerational enough to embrace quite a lot of different themes and emotions and styles. I don't think rock music is just teenage anymore, it's much more than that. I'm interested in the more adult side of rock 'n' roll, if you like, that deals with other emotions, more desperate emotions, more extreme emotions. I think rock music can move towards other forms, like cinema or the novel or poetry or theatre. It can rise up to that level, if people let it."

In an industry filled with raging egos and rampant opportunism, where personal and professional self-indulgence is not only accepted but also encouraged, Richard Thompson is a refreshing breeze. All the more curious given the trials he has been subjected to in public. The death of Fairport Convention singer Sandy Denny in 1978, from a fall down a flight of stairs, likely left permanent scars on Thompson, but he has kept his thoughts to himself. Eyebrows went up and speculation went wild when, on *Shoot Out the Lights*, he wrote a song called, "Did She Jump or Was She Pushed?" The release of that successful album, recorded with his wife Linda, coincided with the bitter breakup of their marriage, a breakup played out on stage. It provided fodder for many an adult rock song on subsequent albums.

Likely much of Thompson's stability comes from his religious beliefs. In the mid-seventies when it seemed the rest of the rock world was either being born again or joining fringe religions like Scientology and the Moonies, he typically went his own way by becoming a Sufi, a branch of Islam. To this day he is still a member. "I've always believed in God," he told me, "and I always wanted to find the best way to express that. It seemed the way that had the most knowledge available and the clearest path, if you like. I grew up as a Christian and I just found very grey areas of Christianity, where people couldn't tell you what the next step was or what was missing. Whereas, in Islam I just found a much more complete picture."

Thompson acknowledged that his religious beliefs influenced his music. "It makes music a lot clearer, and it gives me a map through the shark-infested waters of the popular music world." He paused from his guitar picking, looked up at me, smiled again, then burst into laughter.

7

The
Lion
in Winter

Ask any Canadian to name a famous Canadian poet and the chances are quite good that even those who don't pay attention to poetry will come up with one name: Irving Layton. As a personality, let alone as a poet, he has writ large on the walls of our contemporary history.

I was reminded of this fact in early 1994 when I returned to a place I hadn't been in almost forty years. From 1956 to 1959, I lived in Washington, D.C. — actually just outside the District in a place called Hyattsville. For reasons that have long since vanished in the electric mists of time, I had read during that time Irving Layton's poem "The Improved Binoculars," which described a city in flames, orphans being burned to death, and city fathers pompously indifferent to the carnage. Perhaps I had seen a fire that made the poem more real to me, or perhaps it was just the sheer force of the poetic images on my ten-year-old brain, but it apparently stayed with me all of that time, like a stowaway in the back of my mind.

In 1994, as I stood on a hill overlooking the greenbelt right-of-way that ran behind my old house in Hyattsville — the greenbelt where my father and I had buried my first dog after he had been killed by a car — a line from Layton's poem suddenly came back to me "All this I saw with my improved binoculars." I hadn't read the poem since the fifties, and, despite contact with Layton as a journalist, I had completely forgotten that I had even been aware of his existence thirty-seven years earlier.

I first met Irving Layton when he was seventy-seven years old. It was 1989 and I was astonished to learn that he was actually doing an abbreviated book tour to promote *Wild Gooseberries: The Selected Letters of Irving Layton*, edited by Francis Mansbridge.

Layton had always struck me as somebody who lived his life to the absolute fullest, open to everything, no holds barred, no emotion unfelt, no idea left unexamined, no drink left undrunk, no woman left unappreciated. In 1966 the CBC put out a recording of Canadian poets reading their work and Robert McCormack described Layton in the liner notes with great precision: "It is evidently his conception of his role that he is to be all things to all men: the lover, the clown, the hero, the rebel, the Old Testament prophet, but above all The Poet in the grand old Romantic sense, at once the scourge and comfort and delight of his people."

Mention Irving Layton's name in mixed company and you could still get strong reactions: men tend to like him, and an apparently large number of women seem to regard him as nothing more than a randy old satyr.

The predominant impression, though, was of a man not afraid to take chances, a man disinterested in the prosaic and mundane, a man unconcerned with the type of security most of us seek in our lives.

"I never looked for it," he told me. "I intentionally did everything possible to make it impossible for me to have that kind of security."

"Why?"

"Because I believe in living dangerously, recklessly. I have a line in one of my poems, 'I go about making trouble for myself, the sparks fly, I gather each one and start a poem.' For me, poetry comes out of turmoil, it comes out of conflict, it comes out of dissatisfaction, it comes out of strife and danger. All good writing comes out of suffering. All creativity comes out of suffering. If man was not an animal that suffered, he wouldn't make the magnificent inventions that he's made, nor would he create the tremendous works of art — plays or poems or novels — if he were a complacent pig, or a contented cow."

Hand in hand with Layton's sense of recklessness comes the fatalism of the sceptic.

"I don't have a lighthearted outlook," he said. "This is a century that has given us the most infamous crime ever committed under the light of heaven, namely the holocaust. It has also given us Hiroshima, and it has given us Gulag. These are the most hideous events in human history — there's no comparison to the atrocities committed by twentieth-century man."

Even age, he said, could not temper this feeling. "There's been nothing to mellow me. But I would say that I'm a little more compassionate toward my fellow men because I realize that they are, to a large extent, helpless. Perhaps because of their own doing or undoing, they're caught in toils of economics and sociology and politics, and the average person really has not got much power to change conditions. The individual today does not have the sense of security and power that his forebears had."

This kind of straightforward talk has been as much responsible as his poetry for creating Irving Layton's public image.

Back in 1962, Layton had been one of six poets to read at the legendary Le Hibou coffeehouse on Bank Street in Ottawa. The Wednesday night reading series created some controversy because taxpayer's dollars in the form of a Canada Council grant had been given to pay the poets and cover expenses. For seven nights and seven poets the Canada Council had handed over the princely sum of $600.

It was a bitterly cold evening when Layton read and the line of those waiting to get in wound down the narrow stairway from the second-story club, out onto the sidewalk, and down the street. One lank-haired young woman was quoted in the local press saying, "I knew he was important. Even my mother-in-law has heard of him."

Layton did not disappoint that night. He was fiery and funny, tender and aggressive; he read poems about young women and about life — he even read one about Jackie Kennedy. I know all of this not because I was there — though Le Hibou was my hang-out starting around that time — but because the club's owner, Harvey Glatt, had the evening recorded for later release on record. Twenty-seven years later, Harvey Glatt was the owner of the radio station where I worked and he gave me the master tapes to listen to before I met Layton.

Unlike Leonard Cohen, who had once told me his own poetry "seemed familiar" but he couldn't remember it word for word, Layton had no problem reciting along with the tapes as I played them for him, smiling and nodding as he spoke. I was startled by his memory for his own work — and also by his appearance. Perhaps it was his larger-than-life reputation that led me to expect something different, but Layton is a short, stocky man with a mane of white hair and a pleasant, tanned, and creased face filled with lines that could only have been put there by laughter. He reminded me of nothing so much as an amiable and mischievous leprechaun.

The letters in *Wild Gooseberries* reveal the wide range of Layton's interests and his love of words and phrases, not to mention the absolutely incredible number of people he has corresponded with in his life. "I've written over five thousand letters," he told me proudly. "I'm a freak because letter writing, as you know, has gone out of style. Very few writers today write letters."

But Layton's long friendship with Leonard Cohen is reflected by only two letters, neither of which was answered. Strange, I thought, for two men who craft words for a living.

"We have been great friends for over thirty years," Layton laughed, "but I may have had two small postcards from him in those three decades."

"Were they quality postcards?" I wanted to know.

"Well, I wouldn't say quality."

"Along the lines of 'Irving, it's beautiful here in Greece. Wish you were here.' Something like that?"

"Something like that, yes."

"How did you meet Cohen?" I asked.

"It was about thirty years ago," he recalled. "At that time he was still at McGill — I think he was in his final year. I had brought out a book called, *The Long Peashooter*, so that's around 1953 or '54, and he at that time was the president of his frat and he was very close to his frat brothers —"

I couldn't help but interrupt.

"Leonard Cohen belonged to a fraternity?" I was incredulous.

"Well, that's the patrician in him, you see."

"God, do you suppose he went to toga parties and things like that?"

Layton laughed. "Well, he's never denied it. I don't think he's boasted about it, but he's never denied it either. Anyway, he wanted me to come over and give a reading for his fraternity and that's how I met him."

The start of a long stretch of public recognition for Layton began in the mid-fifties, just about the time the Beats had reached their peak in the United States. During my visit to the Kerouac gathering in Quebec City in 1987, I had come across a series of black-and-white photographs that showed a party in New York City circa 1959, attended by Allen Ginsberg, Lawrence Ferlinghetti, and Irving Layton. He said he had been invited to New York by the publisher Jonathan Williams, whose Jargon Press was reissuing Layton's *The Improved Binoculars*. Jargon Press was dedicated to publishing "maverick poets, stray photographers, oligarchs and characters." William Carlos Williams had written the introduction, and the party shown in the photographs was the book launch.

"They liked my work," he said of the Beats. "I was not that

excited about their work because I felt they had left out things that I like in poetry. I like resonance. I like musicality in lines. Well, they were not as interested as I was in the mating of music to meaning. I'm fanatical about it. I like to see a good resonant line of poetry and it has to be musical. They were not interested in music and that's fine, that's their poetics. So I don't know why they went for my work."

Layton's letters make entertaining reading for many reasons, not the least of which is his vitriol. He is a man capable of towering rage against anyone he believes has slighted him or, for that matter, praised him. In one of his letters he acknowledged that he is quarrelling with everyone and admitted, "I seem to be unable to restrain myself from attacking anyone who ever says a good word about me. That man called me a genius! No punishment can be too severe for him! Right?"

In his introduction to *Wild Gooseberries*, Francis Mansbridge expressed pleasure at Layton's ability "to interweave amazing arrogance with ironic distancing." The man, he said, wears well. Layton himself recognized this when he told me that nobody bore him a grudge because they all realized his anger dissipated quickly.

One passage of particular vehemence appeared in a letter to Peter Gzowski, who had reviewed a collection of Layton's love poems. After he referred to the broadcaster as a "poor discredited shit," Layton ended with, "I shall put all my gifts to work so that of all the noisome insects I've pinned against their own dung, you will always shine with an especial distinction."

"That's beautifully phrased!" he beamed. "I don't think he lost any sleep over it; he shouldn't have anyway. After all, he inspired one of the most brilliant lines of invective — it's magnificent."

In 1992, the author and anthologist John Metcalf edited a collection of Layton's love poems called *Dance with Desire*. Ottawa artist Richard Gorman had been commissioned to create a series of etchings to illustrate the book. Layton was coming to

Ottawa to launch the publication with a public reading, and it would coincide with his eightieth birthday. The owners of the bookstore where the reading would take place were also the owners of an adjoining restaurant of some distinction, and so, the evening prior to the reading, there would be a private dinner to celebrate Layton's birthday. John Metcalf asked if I would like to attend. I agreed but asked if I could record the event for "Medium Rare." I promised the technical equipment would be inconspicuous. I was given approval and was rewarded with one of the most memorable evenings I have experienced, as well as a wonderful "radio vérité" event.

In attendance were Irving Layton and his wife Anna Poittier; John Metcalf and his wife Myrna; the artist Richard Gorman; another artist Fran Hill, accompanied by her young and brooding boyfriend; editor Doris Cowan; my friend Randall Ware from the National Library; Micheline Rochette, who was the official photographer of the event; and myself.

Layton was in an expansive mood, surrounded by admirers and about to be treated to a wonderful meal in his honour. As the cork on the first bottle of Veuve Cliquot popped, he commented that it was "a nice and cheerful noise."

The evening began with a round of toasts to Layton, who, in turn, raised his glass to his wife, Anna, for her "love, compassion, and inspiration." He then proposed a challenge to the table that would be responsible for the progress of the remainder of the evening; he asked each of us to recall some strange and wonderful story, something that had happened to us personally that we could not explain, some odd occurrence, or, better still, some eerie event or coincidence that illustrated the mystery of life.

"Because this is an unusual evening," he said, "where writers and painters and sculptors are getting together. You know, what the hell is literature all about, what the hell is poetry all about if it isn't about a defiance of reality? Reality smells, it stinks, unless it's gotten ahold of by the artists who transmute it into something strange and wonderful. So I want strange stories that show the remarkable and the magical in all our lives. Those of us who are lucky enough to have a line to our childhood know it's there."

As Layton spoke, his wife Anna, sitting beside him, would watch him carefully, picking up his napkin from the floor when it slid unnoticed from his lap, providing an appropriate word when one failed to come to him, or repeating in his ear the words of one of the other guests if Layton failed to hear. Her attention was unobtrusive and not in the least patronizing, which could easily be the case for any other couple whose age difference was nearly fifty years.

(The following evening, prior to the reading, I would get to spend an hour with Anna Poittier at the bar in the restaurant. I would discover a charming and intelligent woman, completely devoted to her husband. The pleasantness of that discovery was only enhanced by my memory of the snide comments and arched eyebrows that I had seen whenever her marriage to Layton was raised in conversation. Poittier herself was certainly not unaware of the raft of speculation regarding the motives of a twenty-year-old marrying a seventy-year-old, but her marriage had endured a decade at that point and showed no signs of waning.)

As the first glasses of champagne were emptied, Layton concluded his remarks on the nature of reality and the artist's role in interpreting it. He announced that he would begin with his own strange story, giving the rest of us time to quell the panic that we would come up short when it was our turn.

"Many years ago," he began, "I found myself in Père Lachaise cemetery in Paris and I knew that Baudelaire was buried there. I've always had a great affection for Baudelaire — I always identified myself with his tormented life and his genius, both. Pardon the vanity, but what the hell's a poet without his vanity?

"So I find myself in the cemetery and I ask somebody there, where is Baudelaire buried? So the person, almost contemptuously, says 'par lo, par lo,' and he waves a hand. So I say, okay, and

I start walking. And I walk and I walk, and here is that strange and eerie and almost incredible thing that happened — and, so help me God, I swear that every word I tell you from here on is the truth.

"I walk on and as I get farther and farther away — and I don't really know where I'm going — I feel a very great sadness, a great heaviness come over me and I can't understand why. I know I'm in a cemetery, but I've been in the cemetery for some time — why suddenly am I feeling sadder and sadder and more and more melancholy with every step that I take?" Layton's voice had risen dramatically at this point and he paused to look around the table. Nobody was moving, nobody was speaking, and one or two champagne glasses were frozen in mid-air, suspended on their way to waiting mouths.

"I keep on and I keep on," he continued, "and my sadness grows. And then, and here's the miraculous thing, just as I was beginning to sob with the heaviness and the sadness, the tears are coming down, and I'm continuing on, and the sobs grow heavier and heavier, and with my last sigh, my last sob — so help me God, it's the truth! — I find myself right there in front of a grave, and I look up and I read, 'Charles Baudelaire.'

"Why did it happen? Was it the tragedy of Baudelaire's life that came to me from the very grave that interred his bones, his ashes? What was it? It is a very incredible and, for me, an inexplicable thing."

Pausing only long enough to have his glass refilled, Layton then asked for someone else's strange story. A quick look around the table showed that nearly everybody had been waiting to see how strange the guest of honour's story was before they began searching their own memories for something similar. Perhaps it was my broadcaster's dislike for dead air, or the fact that I was into my third or fourth glass of champagne, but I stepped into the awkward pause and volunteered my own story.

As luck would have it, my story also involved Père Lachaise

cemetery — where I had gone for the first time with my wife a year earlier — and a visit to the grave of Amedeo Modigliani, the artist. On his tombstone had rested a small rock, holding in place a piece of notepaper. At the top of the paper was drawn a yellow crown, and below, the words, "Amedeo, Forever the King." I was struck by the newness of the note, no sign that it had been there much longer than a day or two, perhaps even placed there earlier that morning.

A few months later, I told the table, I was preparing to interview the Canadian poet Anne Michaels about her collection of poems called *Miner's Pond*. In it, I found a poem entitled, "Stone," written from the point of view of a woman who had spent her life involved with Modigliani. Anne Michaels had described the Paris in which Modigliani lived, his last days of alcoholism, and his desire to sculpt rather than paint, and she referred to him in the poem as "a fallen king." I was struck by the coincidence and assumed Anne Michaels had also been to Paris, and to Père Lachaise, recently. To my surprise, when I asked her, she told me she had never been to Paris in her life. The poem, she said, was a work of pure fiction.

My tale was met with nods of approval around the table, and a murmur of appreciation from Layton. Thank God, I thought, breathing easier and reaching for another glass, now let's see how the rest do.

As I expected, the next brave soul was John Metcalf. His story involved the mysterious attraction he holds for panhandlers everywhere. "I see them half a block away, and they come running — they let thirty people go by, but when it's me, they come."

Metcalf then described an incident in Toronto when a panhandler had swerved through a crowded sidewalk to confront him. "I just kept walking in a straight line, and he just stood there," Metcalf recalled. "And when I reached him he said, 'Good day, sir.' And I said, 'Good afternoon.' He said, 'Would you answer me a question?' I said, 'Certainly,' and he said, 'Would you not

agree that the Irish breed the greatest racehorses in the world?'
And I said, 'I most certainly would!' And he said, 'Well then fuck
you, sir!'"

As the laughter died down, someone asked Metcalf, "Did you
give him any money?"

"I most certainly did not," came the reply.

The evening was now well underway, fine food was served, the
guests were becoming more lubricated, and the conversation was
becoming easier and more animated. Layton pointed out that it
was always a mystery to him why it took drink to make people
drop their pretensions and their preconceptions and really be
honest with one another. It is a state we should all reside in all of
the time, he said, but, if it took drink to achieve it, so be it, and
he raised his glass.

"I have a poem," Layton went on, "called 'Fortuna et Cupidas,'
which, translated into English means, 'Chance and . . .'"

"And Appetite," Anna supplied.

". . . and Appetite.' It is my belief that if you take any person's
life and you draw a graph with one line called 'chance' and one
line called 'appetite,' wherever they intersect, that's where you are.
In other words, each of us is the product of these two forces.
Chance will bring two people together and appetite will continue
the meeting. This is one of my strongest beliefs. I can tell you the
story of my marriages that will illustrate perfectly what I've just
told you.

"So each one of you, if you were to truthfully and honestly tell
the stories of your lives — how you met a certain person or got a
certain job — it would be these two things, chance and appetite,
that were responsible. And this gathering tonight is a perfect
example: chance brought us together, but appetite or desire con-
tinues the meeting.

"I will soon be eighty . . ."

"You are." From Anna.

"Anna is . . ."

Anna smiled. "Thirty-two."

"Thirty-two. I am Jewish — listen carefully, take it in — Anna is an Acadian, a Catholic. In other words, her cultural background is quite different from mine. The disparity in age is quite clear."

All eyes tried not to be on Anna.

"I mean, eighty," Layton shook his head. "A guy of eighty doesn't even dream of an erection anymore, you know."

"Oh, Irving," chided Metcalf, "stop telling these awful lies."

"Surely you dream?" I asked hopefully.

"Irving," offered Richard Gorman, "you won't be eighty until you're a hundred and ten."

"God bless you for saying that," said Layton. "But you would say, if you were a sociologist, that the chances of the two of us having a happy and successful and wonderful marriage that has endured for nearly ten years, would be very slim. Very few would be willing to bank their savings on anything like this.

"Yet here are Anna and I, after ten years, as much in love, if not more, than we were at the beginning. And that's what life is all about, that's what poetry is all about, that's what the poets are always talking about. They're always trying to make people aware that there is magic about, the unpredictable, there's chance and there's beauty and there's love."

More food came, more wine was consumed, and more stories were told. Myrna Metcalf told of a strange visit to Stonehenge; the dishevelled Richard Gorman told a wonderful tale about giving the Rideau River offerings of tobacco, in the Indian fashion, for allowing itself to be the subject of a mural he was painting, and how the ritual had attracted all manner of wildlife to the spot; the brooding boyfriend of Fran Hill told a story that seemed to involve drug use and that weird state of consciousness between sleep and wakefulness, though everyone was too drunk by that time to understand what it was he was trying to say.

Finally, nearly four hours after the meal had begun, Irving Layton raised his hand for quiet.

"I have a feeling, as a poet who has been writing for sixty years," he said, "that every person on this planet believes that he is not understood. That every person feels that the core of him is much more beautiful, much more lovable, much more affectionate than people realize. I'll be quite frank and say that this comes from my own sense that somehow or other my beautiful soul is not understood.

"I like to think there's a buried self in all of us, a child, an adolescent, somebody who's tasted a beauty, or insight, which ordinary life prohibits. And that child is there. And I think Blake is with me, and Shelley is with me, and Wordsworth is with me in expressing just that thought. In our selves there is somebody who is very beautiful and very innocent, who has escaped the corrupting influence of civilization. And that individual is struggling to keep alive, to say: 'you know, the world is really beautiful, there is the colour red, and there is the touch of the hand, and the kiss of the mouth and there are beautiful eyes. And you look into those eyes and you have been profoundly moved. And you have seen sad things, and heard sad songs, and they've touched you as nothing else has.' Remember that. Remember that as you go down the street, and the alley, that sound is there, it's always there. That's the poet. He has some kind of touch, some association with that ghost. And that's what makes him a poet. He's haunted, he's troubled all his life. And all his life, he seeks to release his troubled, imprisoned child, ghost, spirit that is buried within every individual."

After one more round of toasts in his honour, Irving Layton and Anna Poittier gathered their things together and said goodbye. The rest of us lingered over coffee and liqueurs for awhile longer and gradually drifted off.

As I made my way home, I realized how right Francis Mansbridge had been. Irving Layton wears well.

Political Animals

E very weekday for nearly fifteen years, I hosted a one-hour radio program that dealt with the issues of the day, not arts and culture. This current affairs show, called "CHEZ Ottawa," consisted of interviews on the topics in the news that day. But, every so often, some political interview would stray into the area of social significance that made it part of the culture. These interviews usually ended up on "Medium Rare."

The three pieces in this chapter are cases in point. Keith Davey was privy to the inner workings of one of the most fascinating and influential political careers in Canadian history: that of Pierre Elliott Trudeau; René Lévesque will be remembered as one of the country's most impassioned individuals; and journalist John Sawatsky was responsible for the definitive biography on one of Canada's most reviled politicians: Brian Mulroney.

❏

Senator Keith Davey practically filled the studio, he was that large. Not an overweight man — just tall and what my mother always called big-boned.

It was October 1986. Davey was making the rounds with his memoirs. I confess to more of a fondness for political memoirs than journalistic ones; there are only so many times you can hear a reporter talk about where he was when Kennedy was killed.

The Rainmaker: A Passion for Politics told the story of the ultimate backroom boy, someone whose life was so steeped in politics, Liberal politics, that he knew as a boy which houses in his neighbourhood were Grit and which were Tory.

Keith Davey started his career with Lester Pearson and went on to become Pierre Trudeau's political advisor. He had long been regarded as the key Liberal strategist, a man with a Machiavellian turn of mind and a down-home demeanour.

I had spent a good deal of time preparing for my meeting with him, because I saw it as a chance to review some significant turns in Canadian political history over the previous two decades from a totally different perspective. Instead of getting the usual weasel-worded answers from politicians who always have the next election in mind, here was an opportunity to get the straight goods from an insider with nothing to lose. Davey's outspoken chronicle was already getting censured because it suggested that John Turner had real opinions on key issues of the day that he wasn't sharing with the public.

I had prepared a selection of audio clips from over the years that I planned on playing for the senator at different points in the interview, to break up the sound of the two of us talking and to provide jumping-off points for new areas of discussion.

The senator squeezed himself into a chair across the studio table from me. He had a big, deep voice to go with his size, and he was very easygoing and friendly. He told me he had begun writing the book the day Trudeau resigned because he was no longer interested in being a player in the political process. "I don't want to run anymore campaigns," he said. "I've run seven. I'm without guile. I'm being very honest with you. I really am not interested in being a power player. I've done that for a long time and I don't want to do that anymore."

I watched his face closely as I played an audio clip of Pierre

Trudeau's "Just Society" speech. He appeared to be genuinely moved.

"Yes, it almost makes me cry," he said. "I guess I revere Pierre Trudeau and I guess I always will. I think that the things that he set forward in 1968 he by and large achieved. As a backroom guy, I'd have to say that there was one particularly remarkable thing about Pierre Trudeau. You know, Laurier made a speech in Vancouver and they heard about it a day and a half later in Toronto and Ottawa; Trudeau was in everybody's home every single night on the tube. Here's a guy who lasted sixteen years."

Our conversation ranged over a lot of Liberal ground during the next forty minutes. The senator spoke of Trudeau's impressive farewell speech delivered at the Liberal convention in 1984 that was done without notes. He told me how angry he was at singer Paul Anka, who was hired to sing his song "My Way" during the tribute to Trudeau. "The words to that song, that's Pierre Trudeau, that's the way he's lived his life. And I wanted it to be part of the concert segment of the tribute evening. We brought Anka in and he wrote some new words and wrote himself into the song. I thought that was tacky."

Davey also revealed how personally demoralized he felt when John Turner self-destructed during his TV debate with Brian Mulroney, getting eviscerated publicly on the issue of Pierre Trudeau's patronage.

Finally, at the end of the interview, I asked Davey to give me quick thumbnail sketches of various public figures he had dealt with over the years. His frankness was disarming.

On then clerk of the Privy Council Michael Pitfield: "A brilliant and unusual guy. He is the ultimate egghead, and here is the ultimate egghead chewing gum and smoking cigars. He looked like more of a backroom boy than I did!"

On Joe Clark: "I like Joe Clark a lot. He may have lost his luggage, but he never lost his principles. I've always resented the reporter who said I described Clark as a wimp. As I recall, I set the record straight on that one."

On Ed Broadbent: "I like Ed Broadbent — I sound like I like everybody — but I like Ed. I wish he was a Grit. I think he's a very effective guy. He's very smart, though he conveniently ignores the fact that he's owned lock, stock, and barrel by big labour."

I was satisfied with the Keith Davey interview and aired it the day after it was recorded. (I was even more satisfied when, the following spring, I was to win my first National Radio Award for it.)

That self-important glow from believing I had spun out the real Keith Davey for my listeners vanished in an instant when, a few weeks later, I found myself among the reporters at the Liberal leadership convention asking the senator, a Jean Chrétien supporter, if he would wear one of John Turner's campaign scarves.

"I'm not putting on a Turner scarf under any circumstances," Davey huffed. "Not because I wouldn't support John, but because it's silly."

Within two hours John Turner was securely re-established as the Liberal leader with a 77 percent majority.

I encountered the senator coming off the CBC television platform wearing a Turner scarf.

"Senator, what's that around your neck?"

"It's one of the Turner scarves," he answered, looking at me as if I was demented.

"You said you'd never put one on."

"When did I say that?"

"Two hours ago."

"Of course I wasn't going to put one on until after the vote."

"It would just be silly, you said."

"Well, after the vote it wasn't silly," he shot back, not even trying to keep the exasperation out of his voice. "When a guy gets 77 percent, it's not silly." And he turned and stalked away.

As I left the convention that day, deflated beyond description, Keith Davey's words kept reverberating in my mind: "I'm without guile. I'm being very honest with you. I really am not interested in being a power player."

❐

René Lévesque was small. When I met him at the front door of the radio station in November of 1986, about a month after I interviewed Keith Davey, I was startled to realize how short he was. Like everyone else, I always imagine public figures to be taller than they usually turn out to be. René Lévesque loomed large in the pages of Canadian history, but in the flesh he seemed to be just a shade less than my five foot nine.

He greeted me warmly, and, as we walked to the studio, I realized that he was — naturally — smoking a cigarette. Now the rules covering all federally regulated agencies prohibit smoking anywhere on the premises. Add to this our engineer's edict that smoke was bad for the microphones and other equipment, and suddenly I was caught in a dilemma. I was hoping to get a lengthy and intimate interview with Lévesque, and I knew that if I told him he couldn't smoke, not only would he be cranky and uncooperative, but the interview would also probably only last as long as he could hold out for another. On the other hand, if I let him smoke in the studio, I was breaking the law and, far worse, risking the wrath of our engineer.

As we passed my office, I quickly reached in and grabbed an old ashtray filled with paper clips, dumping them into the wastebasket. I handed him the ashtray and held open the studio door. What the hell, I thought, I wasn't going to let an opportunity like this pass by.

In 1986, René Lévesque's autobiography was published in English. The original French title translated as *Wait, While I Remember,* but the English version carried the far more pedestrian title, *Memoirs.*

As a journalist based in Ottawa, I had plenty of occasions to see Lévesque in action, at first ministers conferences and the like, for nearly a decade. While I didn't agree with his political stand on Quebec's place in (or out of) Canada, I had a great deal of admiration for the man; his passion and commitment were right there on the surface, as was his humanity. René Lévesque seemed driven by ideals and beliefs and not by the need to get re-elected. In politics, especially Canadian politics, this was as rare a commodity as you could find. If Pierre Trudeau was brains, René Lévesque was soul.

During the hour we spent together, Lévesque smoked about four cigarettes — I even joked about it during the interview — and later one of the copywriters at the station scooped the butts up in a plastic bag and they were auctioned off to raise money for the disabled.

Lévesque's book was fascinating reading because he spent just as much time writing about his youth in the Gaspé and his life before politics as he did examining the historic political events of which he was a part. He told me he really enjoyed going back in his mind to the days of his youth, trying to rediscover what it was that made Quebec in the thirties a "paradise" for a child.

He talked about how important a role model his father had been for him, even though his father died when Lévesque was just fifteen years old. "As far as I'm concerned today, he was a great man, in many ways."

He said his mother always wanted him to become a lawyer, like his father, and castigated him for going into politics, "such a dangerous and uncertain profession."

Lévesque was a journalist during the Second World War with the American Broadcasting System and he was with the first Americans to reach the concentration camp at Dachau. He said he remembered it as if it were yesterday.

"The whole thing was organized in such a way that was so bloody scientific," he said, exhaling a cloud of smoke. "You can have savagery . . . but well-organized, scientific savagery! What we found was that it was more than just simple hell on earth, it was a sort of well-devised plan to eradicate people little by little, after they had finished working them to death. It was an unbelievable thing."

I asked him what kind of permanent impression was left on him from the experience.

"Well, I remember one day when we were around that crematorium having to go out twice and simply throw up." He paused to light another cigarette. "My cameraman was trying to get a fifteen- or twenty-second segment organized and he couldn't get to the end of it. What it leaves you with is something indescribable, but you realize that if wars can lead to things like that, you become a dedicated pacifist for the rest of your life, that's for sure."

As we spoke, Lévesque sat hunched forward, his head low, his elbows on the table, the cigarette in his left hand waving about as he emphasized a point. I got the impression that we could just as easily have been sitting in somebody's kitchen over drinks late at night, arguing politics and life. It was that informal intensity that made René Lévesque such an appealing public figure.

We talked about Pierre Trudeau, during his *Cité libre* days, who had asked Lévesque if he could write ("I felt like telling him he could go right straight to hell"); about the corruption of Maurice Duplessis ("He reflected a kind of conservatism that most Quebeckers felt at the time"); and about the night in 1976 when the Parti Québécois came to power ("We didn't expect it and it was like, all of a sudden, having one hell of a load shoved onto your shoulders").

But by far the most interesting topic was the October Crisis of 1970, when the FLQ kidnapped British diplomat James Cross and Quebec cabinet minister Pierre Laporte. Lévesque had made the astonishing admission in his book that, at the outset, he considered the incidents to be the actions of some "nervy guys." Did this mean, I asked, that he actually had some admiration for the kidnappers?

"I think everybody did," he answered, "in this sense: obviously the first kidnapping of Cross was nothing that you could endorse, but, on the other hand, it didn't look like it was too dangerous. They were asking for a few things, like all terrorists will — money, the right to get out to some other country, and all of that. But when the answer came from the government, [Jerome] Choquette was the one that was put on the air to say 'no deal.' That was about six o'clock in the afternoon on the Saturday, a week after Cross had been kidnapped.

"And not even an hour later the news comes out they've picked up Laporte, a Quebec minister. Well the first reaction that you had — call them nervy, or what have you — it didn't look like anybody would die, it looked more like some sort of dangerous juvenile stuff. So, yeah, there was a little bit of admiration for the quickness with which they had reacted, but the admiration went very fast after what happened."

Lévesque said that he could never understand why the Liberal government of Pierre Trudeau allowed the FLQ to read its manifesto on the radio because it described the plight of the average Quebecker so precisely that it struck a massive chord.

"The impact was incredible. Without agreeing with what the FLQ was doing, Quebeckers found themselves in agreement with a hell of a lot of the things the FLQ was describing. They had chapter and verse about many of the things that were bitterly resented in Quebec. Ottawa had a shock, because it found out that many of the things it had lost contact with were still very alive in Quebec."

It wasn't only Ottawa that got a shock from the reading of the manifesto; so too did the Parti Québécois and, in particular, René Lévesque. The terrorists mentioned him by name, suggesting they had taken his advice and had worked for the PQ in the 1970 election, only to see a Liberal victory prove the province was just a "democracy of the rich."

Lévesque said he had no way of knowing if these "nervy guys" had actually worked for the PQ during the election, but he realized that he would have to keep a cool head in his daily newspaper column in *Le Journal de Montréal*, particularly since graffiti had begun appearing on walls around the province shouting, "PQ = FLQ."

"In the short term it was murder," he admitted with a shrug. "Our opponents, the Liberals, had immediately — because it's so easy in a panic situation to fudge everything — started the campaign, they never officially endorsed it, on walls all over the place saying, 'PQ = FLQ.' We had to hold tight for dear life for a few weeks. But, curiously enough, it didn't last because people found out that the whole thing had been a manoeuvre. So, finally, when we had a by-election in Laporte's riding after he was killed, we didn't win it, but the same candidate stood for election and had a better score than he'd had a year before. So that meant the race was over."

His fourth cigarette was nearly done and I knew I had only a few more minutes of his time. Lévesque spoke proudly of how Quebec had emerged from a "bootstrap operation" a few decades earlier to become a vital and dynamic mainstream society in 1986.

I asked him if he would be writing in more detail about the historic constitutional conferences in which he had taken part, something less personal and more for the official record.

"I doubt it," he laughed. "I want to write more — I just don't know what yet."

One year after our conversation, René Lévesque was rushed to hospital suffering from "respiratory discomfort." A short time later he died of a massive heart attack.

I thought of the last lines of his book, written in September of 1986, just two months before I met him: "'Thoughts take wing,' writes Julien Green, 'but words travel by foot.' It's midnight. The wing droops, the words crawl. I've almost no more paper and no time left at all."

❏

John Sawatsky is considered by just about everybody in the business of journalism in Canada to be the best investigative reporter around.

The lanky, bearded, and slightly balding journalism professor has built his reputation writing books that range from detailing the workings of the RCMP Security Service to revealing the machinations of Ottawa lobbyists. But nothing added to his credibility more, nor created more controversy, than his biography of Brian Mulroney, *Mulroney: The Politics of Ambition*.

Using his journalism students as researchers, Sawatsky amassed thousands of details on Mulroney's life. These facts were listed on grids of paper that spilled across his classroom walls. When they were assembled, a picture emerged of Mulroney's life, from his boyhood days in Baie Comeau, to the prime minister's residence at 24 Sussex Drive in Ottawa.

The advance word on the book was so intense that when I introduced Sawatsky at an author's breakfast during a mid-summer booksellers' conference, two months prior to its publication, his reading was covered as a news story by the Canadian Press.

Passages dealing with Mulroney's drinking and carousing, the real story on his post-secondary education, and his duplicitous manoeuvring to destroy Joe Clark had generated so much interest that the Mulroney camp began a pre-emptive strike before the book was published, causing the publication date to be moved up.

Leading the attack to discredit the book was Mulroney's old friend and longtime Tory hack, Pat MacAdam. Ironically, MacAdam was one of Sawatsky's sources.

During an extended interview with Sawatsky about the biography, I noted that MacAdam had acknowledged he was operating at the request of the prime minister, and I asked Sawatsky if the fervour of the attack surprised him. He said it did.

"Obviously, they've been working on this for months," he said. "They've managed to get an early draft of a couple of my chapters and they've been circulating that around and they've been going to people in there and getting them to make statements that appear, and I underline the word 'appear,' to contradict things in the book.

"Then, about ten days before the publication of the book, they leak the most damaging parts. So I think this has to be a first in Canadian publishing history, where the aggrieved party leaks the offending passage."

There were three specific sections of the book that Pat MacAdam was claiming were erroneous. The first had to do with Brian Mulroney's involvement in John Diefenbaker's funeral. In the book, Sawatsky claimed Mulroney, who had long since fallen out of favour with Dief, had managed to have the last laugh on the Chief. Pat MacAdam had been in charge of the funeral train that carried Diefenbaker's body across the country to his hometown of Prince Albert, Saskatchewan. Sawatsky wrote that MacAdam got Mulroney a ticket to the funeral; otherwise Mulroney would never have been allowed to attend. Sawatsky's source for this story was Pat MacAdam, who was now saying Mulroney was invited to the funeral and Sawatsky's story was a lie.

"I just checked the list again last night," Sawatsky said with exasperation, "and Mulroney definitely was not invited. MacAdam says Mulroney was an honourary pallbearer. I checked the list — he was not an honourary pallbearer. The only reason Mulroney got in was because he got a ticket from Pat MacAdam, who was the one who told me he gave Mulroney the ticket."

The second passage from the book was one describing an increasingly inebriated and maudlin Mulroney telephoning the newly widowed wife of his friend and mentor, Robert Cliche. Sawatsky told of a rambling Mulroney talking disjointedly about what a wonderful man Cliche had been. MacAdam contended that both Cliche's widow and his son denied the story, going so far as to produce a letter from Nicholas Cliche that, MacAdam said, refuted Sawatsky's claims.

"These are very mischievous statements," Sawatsky smiled wearily. "They can't deny the facts, so they have to be seen to be denying the facts. I've read Nicholas Cliche's statement and there is nothing in there that contradicts anything in the book. When I read the statement, I said, yeah, that's right, I agree with it. That passage in the book, which MacAdam and these people haven't read until now, is actually a very flattering part of the book for Mulroney. It shows that he was concerned, he phoned up Mrs. Cliche three times that night and said how broken up he was that Cliche had died."

The final controversial passage had to do with the potentially explosive "missing year," when Mulroney was a student in the Maritimes. Sawatsky's book alleged that Mulroney spent time in the Victoria General Hospital in Halifax and told nobody about it. The book also recounted the speculation that was making the rounds at the time among Mulroney's fellow classmates as to the reason for the hospitalization, reasons ranging from a urinary tract infection to venereal disease.

Pat MacAdam was vigorously maintaining that Mulroney had never been a patient at the Victoria General and that a statement from the hospital indicated clearly there was no record of Mulroney having been there.

"There is a one-line statement put out by the hospital, under pressure from the prime minister," Sawatsky countered, "saying that they have no records of him being there. Well, they could have asked me that six months ago and I could have told them there are no records. They could have asked Claire Hoy, who did a book on Mulroney four years ago, and he would have said there are no records in there. We know that. All that means is that record no longer exists there. It doesn't mean he wasn't a patient.

"I interviewed at least two people who visited him in the Victoria General Hospital at the time. I also have a memo written to explain why Brian Mulroney, in the late winter of 1960, could not attend a Progressive Conservative Student Federation meeting because he was in hospital for 'minor surgery.'

"So there's no doubt Mulroney was in the hospital and it's just something that's too embarrassing for him to admit. So they have to come up with this mischievous statement that makes it sound as if they're denying the facts in the book, which they're not denying."

Everywhere John Sawatsky went that autumn of 1991 on his interview tour, there was Pat MacAdam dogging his footsteps. Finally, Sawatsky said, as he was being ushered out of the studio after an interview on the CBC program, *The Journal*, he ran into MacAdam on his way in for his own interview. He decided to confront MacAdam on his allegations, but Mulroney's friend just lowered his head and kept walking into the studio.

Despite the efforts of Pat MacAdam, and, one assumes, Brian Mulroney, to discredit John Sawatsky's book, the biography went instantly to the top of the bestseller lists.

In June of 1993, in the final days before his exit as prime minister, Brian Mulroney went on a Senate-packing spree similar to the one he criticized his Liberal predecessors for carrying out. His old friend Pat MacAdam, the point man for Mulroney's reputation, did not receive an appointment.

9

Women
Who Run
with
the Words

Robertson Davies is fond of saying that Canadians have little appreciation of the esteem with which other nations regard Canadian writing. Whether this is true might be open for argument but, if it is, a corollary could be that foreigners also see Canada as a place to come in order to create good writing.

Both writers in this chapter have begun their lives elsewhere, come to Canada, and have remained here to generate some of the best novels and short stories Canadian literature has seen.

In April of 1995 Carol Shields won the Pulitzer Prize for fiction. It was the latest in a string of accolades the Winnipeg writer had received for her remarkable novel *The Stone Diaries*. Media reports persisted in referring to the Pulitzer as the most "prestigious" literary prize in North America (the latent Canadian inferiority complex that always bubbles to the surface in the face of American recognition), but they seemed to be forgetting the Governor General's Award for English Fiction (which Shields won in 1993), and a nomination for the Booker Prize, the Commonwealth's literary award (also in 1993).

Carol Shields was eligible for the Pulitzer because she has both American and Canadian citizenship. She was born in the United States but moved to Ottawa with her Canadian husband in 1957.

Since 1980 she has lived in Winnipeg, and *The Stone Diaries* is very much a reflection of her own experience. The novel chronicles nine decades in the life of a woman named Daisy Goodwill, who is constantly crossing back and forth over the Canada–U.S. border, between Manitoba, Indiana, and Ontario.

In the late fall of 1992 Shields came to Ottawa for the launching of the Carleton University Press publication of her book of poetry, *Coming to Canada*. I recorded an evening of her reading from the book to an appreciative audience at a local bookstore, then met her in the studio the following day for an interview.

I asked her how much of her own life and memories went into her poems and stories. She smiled. "You know, people sometimes say to me, 'when are you going to write about yourself?' This is what these poems are; they are a sort of biographical fiction that I have put together and I've tried to talk about some of the moments of my life. I've always found it a strange paradox that the two most important ceremonies of our lives — birth and death — are the two during which we are largely unconscious. We like to think that we will meet death full of consciousness — one always thinks of Oscar Wilde's last words, 'either that wallpaper goes or I do' — but one of these poems is an attempt to imagine my own birth. Because I don't remember much about it, I had to fill it in with family legends. I knew the hospital I was born in; I passed it every day on the way to school. I knew that the family had forgotten the name of the doctor and this seemed to me, as a child, to be a monumental slippage of knowledge. The other thing about my birth was that my mother, in describing it, always said — to my enormous embarrassment — 'and she slipped out like a lump of butter!' So all of these things entered into the poem."

Like many writers, Shields augments her own memories with pieces from the lives of others — friends, even strangers. "I think it's universal: the writer's guilt of being a scavenger. A lot of it is eavesdropping, going silent at parties and listening to what other people say, and it's hard to get away from that feeling of using other people's material. But I do, and I'm always conscious of what you do to your own memories. How faithful should you be to them?" She said she worried about becoming too maudlin when she attempted to recreate experiences from her own past in fictional form. "I suppose you don't owe your own memories anything, but the fear is that you will sentimentalize, you will extrapolate falsely from those memories and, once you do that, you lose hold of what you've left behind."

Having this Shields interview on tape gave me the opportunity to review it after Shields rocketed to fame with *The Stone Diaries*. One of the early passages in that book describes a very young Daisy Goodwill lying sick for weeks in a darkened room, hearing only the sounds of life going on outside the window and door, imagining what is happening, and attaching her own fevered embellishments to them. For Carol Shields, memory is like that: distorted, enhanced, and altered with each passing year and with each retelling.

"I was speaking to a poet friend who said, 'I have to go to England because I'm writing a book of poems about my childhood and I have to verify certain events.' It made me laugh because, in fact, the memory you have *is* the true account, to a certain extent. So what is truth? What is the accurate picture? I think it has to feel right psychologically, and I think you do know when you're using it. I also think it's an interesting moral question."

Like the belief in some primitive cultures that the strength of a person's soul is diminished each time their photograph is taken, Shields believes that the meaningfulness of a memory is lessened each time it is recounted. "I think it has to dilute it," she told me. "I suppose that by dragging out your memories, as we do when we sit around talking to friends, we drag them out so often and we polish them up, and fill them in, and they become little set pieces rather than memories. I think they travel a long way from that true memory."

Shields maintains that she can remember her first conscious memory; she knows which memory is her chronological first.

"I find that astonishing," I said to her. "My memories are such a jumble that I'm almost convinced what I think is my first memory happened when I was nine . . . I'm not even sure. How do you feel so certain?"

She laughed. "I'm so certain because . . . you know how people often say, 'I'm not sure if I was told about this event or if I really remember it?' . . . I'm sure it's true because I was alone, and I remember saying to myself, 'I am three years old and I am doing this.' So I'm positive."

Like all good writers, Carol Shields also has an interest in what she calls the "mystery" of acquiring language — how we learn to put names to things and when that process happens. I told her how my two-year-old son pushed the language into new shapes when he called hot air balloons "skyballs" and hummingbirds became "honeybirds." It then made perfect sense when, seeing tadpoles for the first time, he called them "honeyfish" because they were small and quick.

"I think children use language very creatively," she smiled. "It's not that I think that out of the mouths of babes come gems, but that children, out of a kind of innocence, put a particular torque on language that we find surprising; [they have] an odd gift for metaphor which many of us would like to go back to. I don't think that any of us know exactly how language is acquired — it's still a mystery, you know?"

Shields's "mystery" was to be explored in *The Stone Diaries* when Daisy Goodwill's father, Cuyler, is transformed over the course of a decade from a taciturn stonecutter into a loquacious businessman. "That silver tongue — how was it acquired?" Shields writes. "The question — would anyone disagree? — holds a certain impertinence, since all of us begin our lives bereft of language; it is only to be expected that some favoured few will become more fluent than others, and that from this pool of fluency will arise the assembly of the splendidly gifted."

For many people, age brings with it a rigidity of thinking, an abandonment of that creative use of language, but Shields believes there are ways to prevent that from happening. "The old idea of rhyming poetry — we haven't had much rhyming poetry for a hundred years — but this is what champions of rhyme say: that one of the good things about rhyme is that it leads you away from the obvious language cluster that you might be in, into something else, and maybe into a more interesting area."

Novelist, poet, essayist, short story writer, playwright, Carol Shields has tried her hand at all of them. I was curious how she decided which of those forms an idea would take.

"You know, I don't make that decision. I never sit down and say, 'I think this material is suitable for a novel, or suitable for a play.' I guess this comes from my non-linearity," she laughed. "I seem to be not a very decisive person — I kind of float a little bit. I suppose I would think that I'm a novelist more than any other kind of a writer. I'm happiest when I'm writing novels; novels are loose, baggy things, and you can wander all over in them. But there is sometimes material that doesn't fit very well, material that is more speculative. And that's material that I will make a note of, and think, 'Oh, I'd like to do a short story on that some-day.' As far as writing plays, sometimes someone comes along and says, 'Look we'd like you to do a play for us, and somehow it hap-pens. You find yourself, foolishly perhaps, shaking your head and saying, 'Alright, I'll do it.'"

Despite her predilection for novel writing, Shields began in her late twenties and early thirties as a writer of poetry. She still remembers the satisfactions it provided. "In many ways it was the happiest writing period of my life. There is something about writ-ing a poem and having it come out right, that you're never going to do with a novel. You can never get a whole novel right, and you know it's not right. But sometimes you do feel that you've done a poem that is perfect, that every syllable is in its perfect place, and it's tremendously rewarding: the total capture of an experience. And since that early writing of poetry, I've simply had occasional spurts of going back to it. *Coming to Canada*, which is eighteen years after my last book of poetry, is an accumulation of those little spurts of poems."

❐

Like Carol Shields, Audrey Thomas was also born and raised in the United States but immigrated to Canada's west coast in 1959. From her home on Galiano Island, she proceeded to write a stream of award-winning novels and short stories, and innumerable radio plays.

I met Audrey Thomas for the first time in 1993 when she came to Ottawa as part of a tour to promote her most recent novel *Graven Images*. Reading to an audience the night before our interview, she joked that she recently had been given a mood ring but decided not to wear it when she was in public. In my studio the next day, I commented on this missing ring. "No, I don't wear it," she laughed. "When I did this reading at Harbourfront in Toronto, I looked down and it was black! Right in the middle of the reading! So I turned it around so I couldn't look at it. I mean, tense and anxious is one thing, but *despair*, which is what the black is . . . it was a bad mistake."

Audrey Thomas is one of those people who seems instantly likeable and down-to-earth, as my mother would say. Within moments of meeting her, we were joking around like old friends and I think, if the opportunity had presented itself in the studio, I wouldn't have thought twice about cracking open a couple of beers — it was that comfortable. Which is even more remarkable since I don't drink beer, so there you are.

I suppose, as well, that I was made comfortable because radio is a spoken medium and I can instantly recognize people who are at ease in conversation. So I wasn't surprised to learn how Audrey

Thomas went about writing dialogue for her novels. "I say every-thing out loud," she answered. "I write my books out loud. I often write them into a tape recorder and play them back, because I write longhand. So I want to sometimes have it a little crisper and it lets me hear what it sounds like. When you write longhand you will have a long line, but perhaps when it's printed it will be broken up, smaller. And I do a lot of radio drama . . . I have written twenty-three radio plays for the CBC . . . and I think that has really helped my dialogue."

"It tightens things up?" I asked.

"Absolutely. Think about radio: it's fatally easy to turn off; you can't flip the pages back; you've got to make the listener 'see' the first time around. My writing has always been visual — I'm a frustrated visual artist — but my dialogue has become much, much tighter."

The fact that Thomas writes her work in longhand does not make her an exception in the world of novelists. I have discovered over the years that a great many of them prefer longhand over typewriters or computers. Author John Metcalf once told me that if he couldn't actually feel the words travelling through his hand into the pen and onto the page, he would have no idea what he was writing. Yet to write an entire novel in longhand requires not only patience but also penmanship, neither of which many of us have in abundance.

"I write really fast," Thomas said. "I would have made a good court reporter. It's absolutely legible and I copy it out again, when I give it to a typist."

She said her love of longhand writing was related to her frustrated artistic tendencies. "I was on some panel years ago," she said, "and I mentioned that I really wished I could draw. Someone said to me, 'well, of course, writing longhand you are drawing — you're drawing the line, you're drawing out the words.' I certainly like the very visceral feeling of being connected with the paper."

Not being a slave to writing technology had another, more practical aspect that also appealed to Thomas. "I don't like to travel with anything that can be stolen, other than my passport. So I buy notebooks in the country that I'm in, or the city that I'm in, and they're also kind of a recollection. I've got an amazing collection of notebooks from all over."

Audrey Thomas's notebooks are a record of the same kind of random snippets of other lives that Carol Shields gathers at parties. "It's literally a notebook — it's the names of streets, it may be a tiny bit of conversation that I overhear, it may be music, something like that. My short stories are often set in other countries, and I'll have the name of the cola that they're drinking, stuff like that. And those small details will bring back a whole scene to me. For instance, you travel in West Africa and you go through so many towns where there's an avenue of liberation, in French or English depending on what part of Africa you're in, and you think, 'oh yeah, right! These countries are all ex-colonies and there was a point where they became liberated, they became self-governed.' That's interesting stuff."

Thomas's notebook observations also extend to the people around her. "I notice the way people use their hands. For instance, there are a lot of women who, when they talk to you, twist their wedding rings around." She grinned. "I find that a very interesting gesture. Is that reassurance? Or are they trying to get them off? I mean, why are they doing this thing? I like watching people's hands particularly because I think your hands often give you away. But I usually make my notes after the fact. Particularly if they're personal — if I'm watching somebody's hands or I'm jotting down a bit of dialogue. I won't usually do it while I'm in the presence of the person."

Keeping detailed notes on the words and mannerisms of other people is one thing, but Thomas is not able to keep a written record of her own experiences for possible future use. "I can't keep a diary for lots of personal reasons," she admitted. "I've never quite understood the keeping of a diary, although I like to read Victorian diaries. But to me it's like talking to the person in the mirror. You may do that in the morning, say, 'hello, you look stupid today!' But to actually sit down at the end of the day and say, 'Dear Diary . . . ,' you know? I simply cannot do it."

As critical as dialogue to the success of a novel or short story is the careful and crafted use of images — sharp, clear, and often brief descriptions that set a scene with the fewest number of words. It is here that Audrey Thomas's notebooks full of facts and observations do their job. "The last scene in *Graven Images* is with these children running in a thunderstorm, which has killed six cows. There are these six dead cows in the field. And I could see this scene so clearly when I was writing it, and then I thought, 'okay, this is supposed to be about 1910.' And I saw the raindrops coming down, and these kids running like crazy with this lightening and this thunder. And I said the raindrops were as big as dollars, because the dollars were still big, round things. This is how the kids might have seen them. But what would we say now? Big as loonies? It doesn't have the same ring."

The painstaking job of writing longhand, the polishing of dialogue aloud, the quest for the perfectly succinct image all suggest a writer with a high level of self-expectation. I asked Thomas if she was ever satisfied with her work once it was done. She began shaking her head before I was finished the question. "Never, never, never, never," she laughed. "There is no ideal book. It's like Descartes said, our imperfect world posits the idea of perfection; you can't have a concept of perfection without imperfection."

1.0

The Predator
and
the Poet

"The things that I've put in this book I've never talked to anybody about. I've never talked to my wife, never talked to my kids, never talked to my sisters about it." Christopher Ondaatje leaned his angular frame forward in the studio chair, as if it took effort to get the words out. "I never talked to my brother Michael, who wrote about it. But he was only two years old at the time and didn't go through this agony that we went through. So it was a very personal thing. This image that I had was only in myself. This shame that I carried was only in myself."

It was the spring of 1992 and Christopher Ondaatje, a self-described "predator" in the world of Canadian business, was talking about his revelatory book, *The Man-Eater of Punanai*. The book was extraordinary because, unlike his brother Michael, Christopher Ondaatje had made his mark in the cold-blooded world of business, noted for his ruthless abilities as an unflinching hardball player. He had amassed a fortune by dealing in the stock market and by creating what one observer called "arcane and lucrative" investment devices. He had also written three historical books, been a member of Canada's 1964 gold-medal-winning bobsled team, and sailed, golfed, and played cricket. If his name was mentioned in the presence of most business journalists, lips would curl.

Yet *The Man-Eater of Punanai* was a very personal voyage into Ondaatje's past and the discovery of a family secret that caused him to reassess his feelings about his own father. Family history, and his brother Michael's semi-fictional accounting of it in *Running in the Family*, had led to a rift between them.

"Jesus, don't ask either of them about any of it," advised a friend at the CBC when I mentioned I would be talking with both Ondaatjes within weeks of each other. "Not only won't they appear anywhere together, they won't even talk about it!"

This warning had come a bit too late since I had already talked with Christopher Ondaatje by that time and he had done nothing but speak about his family's past. Not being someone who pays a lot of attention to the business world, I was in possession of just two facts about him: he was the older sibling of a writer I admired, and he had sold off most of his business interests to pursue his passion for wildlife and to return to his native Sri Lanka. At the time he did this he said, "All this share-shuffling, these paper pyramids we are creating, I'm sick of all that, it's not fun anymore."

The Man-Eater of Punanai is the true story of a leopard that had terrorized a village at the turn of the century in what was then known as Ceylon. But it is also the classic story of a son coming to terms with the memory of a dead father he has long forsaken.

The Ondaatjes were a rich and privileged family with a 350-year history in Ceylon. Much of their wealth was amassed by Ondaatje's grandfather and then lost by his father in four short years between 1947 and 1951. "He got into very deep financial difficulties. They said he was a gambler and a hard drinker, this was all true," Ondaatje told me. "When I was young I didn't think about it. But now, having been westernized and understanding the real world as it is, I know that he knew he lived in a pampered society and when things went totally wrong he couldn't hack it. He wasn't prepared. He wasn't tough enough to face the music when things turned against him."

After the family split up, Ondaatje's mother took her children to England, ran a boarding house, took in lodgers, and scrubbed floors — all so they could have a roof over their heads. While his father "steeped himself in alcohol" back in Ceylon, she was raising them to believe they could do anything they wanted in life.

"I was shoved off at twelve years old to go to school in England. I had to start all over again. At seventeen I was kicked out of school because we couldn't pay the bills and I had to start all over again in the city of London. And then at twenty-two, I decided I wasn't going back to Ceylon. I came to Canada and started all over again. I'd given myself a pretty good international education, I'd toughened myself up, I'd learned to be incredibly independent because I did this all by myself."

Thirty-four years later, he returned to Sri Lanka, an ex-colonialist and expatriate, to research the legend of the man-eating leopard. In doing so, he said, he discovered something about himself.

"Here was this other predator in the world of business, this loner, this stalker, this hunter. A lot of myself came out and a lot of my own self-discovery." He also found himself admiring his father for having remained in Ceylon. "There weren't any similarities with my father because he didn't have to go out on his own. He could have . . . perhaps . . . but I think that remaining there was a tough decision."

Yet thirty-four years of shame and anger towards his father's memory had given him an indelible picture of the man.

"The further you go away — you're twelve years old and you never see the man again — the further you go away, and things are going badly, this image of my father becomes a spectre, it becomes an ogre. He is a charismatic and tyrannical man, very dominant, and you build this false image of somebody who has wrecked everything for you, a selfish person steeped in alcoholism, on and on and on."

With the clarity that only the passage of time affords, Ondaatje's trip back to Sri Lanka helped him realize his father was a perfectly normal human being with perfectly normal failings. Then, he said, came an astonishing discovery: the massive debts his father had incurred, which the family had always assumed were used to buy alcohol and pay gambling losses, had actually gone to pay for Ondaatje's education.

"The incredible amounts of money that he spent, even borrowed to spend, a lot of that was spent on my education in England," Ondaatje said with wonder still in his voice. "So the question I have to ask myself is: that gamble on me, was that worth it? Then you have to live with this answer. So this is a wonderful thing to go back and have this one-on-one with your father, even though he's dead, to discover his motives.

"I understand my father now. I understand myself now. So the resolution part of it is that I must understand my children now. I must understand their own desire to stand on their own two feet, their own independence. I cannot rule the world from the grave."

In August of 1993, not long after my conversation with Christopher Ondaatje, the *Globe and Mail* reported that Ondaatje Corp. had acquired a 111-year-old conglomerate in Sri Lanka. The story referred to Ondaatje's "fire-and-brimstone sermon to shareholders" and quoted him saying that he "remains convinced that the welfare state as we know it will bankrupt North America." In September 1994, the *Report on Business* magazine ran a feature on Christopher Ondaatje's investment gambles in his native country, saying that during the trip to Sri Lanka, about which he had spoken to me, he had "marvelled" at the business opportunities. I was left wondering which Christopher Ondaatje was the real one.

Yet if the elder Ondaatje brother is something of a puzzle, the younger brother is a full-blown enigma.

❐

A few months after my talk with Christopher, Michael Ondaatje made headlines by co-winning the prestigious Booker Prize in Great Britain for his novel, *The English Patient.*

Mindful of my CBC friend's warning about the tensions between the siblings, I decided to focus my interview with Michael Ondaatje totally on his writing. I was already halfway through the new novel and, in the few weeks remaining before the interview, I decided to re-read as many of his earlier works as I could, along with some that I had never read. It was a daunting prospect to have to consume so much good writing on a deadline without being able to savour it, but I was helped by one of those bits of serendipity that drop in your lap every so often.

Around this time I had been listening exclusively to a new recording by Dr. John called *Going Back to New Orleans*. I have long had a fascination with the Crescent City and I was also a longtime fan of Mac Rebbenack, the redoubtable Dr. John. One of the traditional songs on the album was a rendition of "I Thought I Heard Buddy Bolden Say," a tune I seem to remember Geoff Muldaur doing back in my folkie days in the sixties.

About a week before the interview with Michael Ondaatje, I took a brief break from reading *The English Patient* and, on a whim, pulled down from my bookcase a copy of the Fall 1983 edition of *Descant*, a publication devoted to poetry, prose, and literary criticism in Canada. The only reason I owned it was because an old friend had a poem published in that edition, a poem I hadn't read in some years. I decided to take another look at it, to see how well it stood up. I was astonished to find that, aside from my friend's poem and a few others, the rest of the paperback-sized book was devoted to Michael Ondaatje's most recent novel at that time, *Coming Through Slaughter*.

This was one of the few Ondaatje works I hadn't read and here were four or five detailed, scholarly pieces evaluating it. Within minutes I realized that the subject of *Coming Through Slaughter* was the very man I had been listening to Dr. John sing about for weeks: Buddy Bolden. As Woody Allen would say, "go figure."

Unlike his brother, Michael Ondaatje is not thin and angular, though I am left with the impression that he is tall. I confess that when we met he reminded me of a younger version of the Canadian actor John Vernon, but with a better complexion.

I asked him if he had heard the Dr. John album. He said he hadn't and we spent some time talking about New Orleans jazz and our impressions of the city. He told me that a number of respected jazz musicians had done an album some years earlier based on *Coming Through Slaughter* and he offered to give me the details so I could get it.

I told him I wanted to talk about Buddy Bolden first, before we got into *The English Patient*, and he agreed. It was at this point that I learned for the first time a very interesting fact about Michael Ondaatje's writing: it's far more spontaneous and far less researched than many of his admirers might think.

I asked him how he came to write about Buddy Bolden.

"I was living in London, Ontario, and I read a brief article which said he'd gone mad in a parade," Ondaatje replied, "which seemed like this very strange private act in a very public place. That by itself fascinated me, and I've always had a great passion for jazz, especially the New Orleans period, so I started to try to research Bolden at that time, which was 1970 or '71, something like that.

"I did the research and started the book with the bare bones of the plot, really, and had to improvise a lot because there wasn't that much about him."

I told him about discovering the edition of *Descant* and I quoted from a piece in it by Sam Solecki that said, "Ondaatje and Bolden cannot think of art without a concomitant imagery of death: the artist as gunman, as spider . . . as cage-maker, as necrophiliac, as insurance executive, as collector, as editor, as suicide."

"Well, necrophiliac's going a bit far, isn't it?" he laughed. "I don't think I have too much necrophilia in my work. I think Sam Solecki has an odd sense of humour, but actually it may be true. It's very difficult for me to step back and look at my books thematically. For me, when I'm writing the books, and even when

I'm remembering the books, what I remember are the individuals in the book, the characters. It's like certain people in a certain house you go to. In *Slaughter* I meet Bolden and the others.

"So that kind of discussion about the thematic or the structural thing in a book tends to leave me cold, because that's not what governs us as human beings. Art and death are always there in our lives but that's just because we're mortal.

"I think in *Coming Through Slaughter* certainly that element was there with the character of Bellocq, who was photographing prostitutes and was very aware of death because of his illness. And Billy the Kid . . . if you see Billy the Kid as an artist then, of course, you have to link up art and death. But I see Billy the Kid as a gunman and that's it, not as an artist."

I confessed to Ondaatje that the extent of the learned discourse on his writing sometimes left me speechless. I showed him one of the pieces in *Descant* that involved an examination of "the morphology of the geography" of the French Quarter in New Orleans where Bolden lived. I asked Ondaatje if he, like me, sometimes felt this material went over the top.

"Listen," he answered, smiling widely, "I got fired from a university because I didn't have a Ph.D., so I'm on your side. I think as a writer it can be kind of overwhelming to read this stuff about your own work. I'm not being critical about this kind of writing because, obviously, it seems valid to an academic, but if you start reading all your reviews and all the things you're supposed to mean, you'd go crazy, I think. So I just don't read that stuff."

I suggested that academic examination, even more so than popular criticism, could have a disabling effect on a writer's output after awhile.

"Oh yeah, I think that's absolutely true," he agreed. "And I think you'd become incredibly self-conscious. When you're starting a new book, the last thing you want to be is self-conscious or even be aware of a readership out there. But to have a readership plus several critics waiting to pounce . . . ," he drew back in mock alarm, laughing. "That's why I put it out of my mind. You really want to forget everything that you've done in the past, you're beginning a new story so you start from scratch again."

Ondaatje revealed that he still wrote in longhand with a fountain pen, shunning the word processor. This gave me an opening into the area of research and, using the detailed description of the bomb disposal methods in *The English Patient*, I asked how much he did before that fountain pen touched the paper.

"I don't do any research, actually," he replied. "If I do research, I do it as I'm writing. I'll give you an example, going back to *In the Skin of a Lion*, which was a book about Toronto and involved the building of the bridge. When I was writing the book I had been circling around this bridge — the Bloor Street Viaduct — which I'd always been fascinated by. So I tried to find out about the bridge and how it was built, but I'd already begun to write about the building of the bridge and then I started to do the research. So the research tends to happen alongside the actual writing."

"So you're doing research on just what you need to know to write it?" I asked.

He nodded. "At that moment, usually. In the meantime, I may have read up on the labour movement in the 1920s, or something like that, so that would have sparked my interest.

"In that book, what became fascinating was when I tried to do research on the building of the bridge, there were absolutely no newspaper articles about who the people were who were building the bridge. There was nothing. Then, when I went to the archives, there was piles of stuff on how much cement was used, how much sand, but nothing about who was building the bridge. So I finally went to the multicultural archives in Toronto and found old interviews and stuff like that.

"But the building of the bridge, and the defusing of bombs in this new book, I had to learn as I was writing it, and that creates a kind of tension for me in the actual writing of the text."

The English Patient tells the story of a nurse, a Canadian soldier, a bomb-disposal expert, and an enigmatic, badly burned patient in a partly demolished convent in Italy at the end of the Second World War. Both the nurse and the soldier are characters from *In the Skin of a Lion*. I asked Ondaatje if he had ever carried characters from one book to another before.

"I've taken very small things from book to book, which haven't even been found by those critics, actually," he smiled. "So I have this theory that you take a little yoghurt and take it to the next book and that grows.

"But I was very uncertain about taking two characters from the other book — I hadn't planned to do that at all. When I finished *In the Skin of a Lion* I thought, okay, that's it, those are the people and I don't fully know what's going to happen to them, but that's the end of the book. Then, when this book began, I rediscovered that the nurse was Hana very gradually, and I was fascinated by that possibility but nervous about the whole idea of a sequel, which I don't like. But they seemed to be so different from the previous book that it was okay. Because in the intervening years of the war, both Hana and Caravaggio had altered emotionally and physically in terms of character, so that it was like drawing a new portrait."

Ondaatje told me that most of his time is spent rewriting. *The English Patient*, he said, took five years from start to finish and three of those were spent writing the story to the end, while two were spent reshaping, reworking, and "tightening it up." The final few months of writing were the worst.

"That last three or four months is so intense," he said. "Your real life is completely lost. You're just obsessed with the balancing out, the phrasing, little details, punctuation, repetition, should this character be held back three more pages — really absurd things. It's like doing a painting and having to decide where the frame ends and that sort of thing. So by the end of it, you never want to read that book again. You might wait ten years and go back and read the whole book, but that's it."

At the time of our interview, it had just been a few weeks since Ondaatje had won the Booker Prize — along with Barry Unsworth — and two weeks later he would win the Governor General's Award for English Fiction. Nearly a year later he would win the best book award in the Canadian and Caribbean division of the Commonwealth Writers' Prize.

I was curious if he thought that the glittering, hyperbole-laden publicity surrounding such events and even the awards themselves were appropriate things for writers to be involved with.

"They're appropriate in the sense that if they're there to publicize books, that's great," he answered. "But if they're there to publicize authors and to create huge vendettas, which is also there, then it's a problem.

"In England it's quite remarkable the effect of the Booker: everyone knows who's on the short list, they go around and they bet and all this nonsense."

The contest for the Booker Prize in 1992 had been characterized by some very bitter acrimony and I asked him if that feeling was evident at the awards ceremony.

"Well the actual event was, unfortunately, a bit like that," he said, "because there weren't too many writers there. The only writers that were there were against you," he laughed. "There were six writers and I'd met some of them before. I love Ian McEwan's book, and I'd met Patrick McCabe who wrote *The Butcher Boy* — in fact, I bet on him.

"I felt quite casual about the whole thing, I felt quite genial about it all. I thought it was quite an honour to be short-listed and that was enough. But when you got into that hall and you had about two hours of dinner and so forth to wait for, then you suddenly had the sense of being watched and that changed it into something else — it wasn't literary anymore.

"But how do you pick one book out of six? It's sort of difficult." He laughed. "So they picked two, I guess."

11

The Ego
Has Landed

My experience interviewing creative people has taught me that most of them are pleasant, genial, and generous. In fact, it seems evident that true talent and true greatness carry with them a modesty that borders on self-doubt. But, every once in awhile, sometimes when pushed and sometimes not, some of these talented individuals can bristle with hubris.

All three people in this chapter were prodded by me into reacting. Two of them I liked, one I didn't.

❏

I interviewed Robertson Davies for the first time in 1985, when he published, almost simultaneously, *The Papers of Samuel Marchbanks* and the second volume of his Cornish Trilogy, *What's Bred in the Bone.*

I remember going out to the reception area of the radio station to greet him and discovering three girls — about fourteen or fifteen years old — clustered around him, getting his autograph. This was not some adolescent rock star, but the Grand Old Man of Canadian Literature.

In physical appearance, Robertson Davies ("Rob" to his friends, a diminutive that has always struck me as strangely inappropriate.

Does this man look like a "Rob"?) is reminiscent of a cross between Monte Woolley in *The Man Who Came to Dinner* and Edmund Gwenn in *Miracle on 34th St.* With his long beard, mane of white hair, and patrician demeanour, it's easy to see why Davies strikes such a chord in so many readers. He looks like what a serious and respected author — or God — should look like.

As we walked to the studio on that occasion, I asked him if the autograph request was something that happened to him often.

"Oh yes," he replied, without any air of self-importance.

My second meeting with Davies came a few years later. It was just a week after I had met and interviewed the writer and anthologist John Metcalf, whose hobby horse is railing about the subsidization of Canadian literature. Metcalf had savaged Robertson Davies, suggesting that Davies was a boring writer with an undeserved reputation. I decided to try out these comments on Davies himself.

The occasion for the second interview was the publication of *The Lyre of Orpheus*, the third volume of The Cornish Trilogy. I began by asking him if there was some special attraction for him to the form of the trilogy, since he had written two others, The Salterton Trilogy and The Deptford Trilogy.

"There isn't any attraction about it, particularly," he replied, "except that I seem to think of long stories which emerge in about three books. If they came out in a single book, it would be a very fat book and a nuisance." Despite this, he said, he did not plan out the story line through three books, but rather the second book came out of the writing of the first, the third out of the second.

I asked him about criticism of his work, quoting a review of the new novel by Janice Kulyk Keefer that was tepid in its praise.

"Well I haven't seen that, you see. I haven't read it and I don't know anything about it and really, critics have to say their say and they always want to find something that they can be doubtful about, you know?

"You can't worry too much about it," he went on. "If you

worried about critics, as Thornton Wilder said, they'd get into your head and they'd write your next book and that would be the end of you. If they know so much about writing, why don't they write something original themselves?"

John Metcalf had written many original stories and he had an opinion of Davies's work, I told him. Would he like to hear some of that opinion? Davies murmured his assent and I snapped on a cassette with this excerpt from the interview with John Metcalf.

"I find his books stultifyingly boring, personally," Metcalf's piercing British accent filled the studio. "The particular book of his that prompted me to make that remark was called *The Rebel Angels*. I thought it was just appallingly written and excruciatingly boring. Everybody has praised it, from coast to coast and in the United States and in England, and I simply cannot understand it. I really found it a great struggle to get through to the end.

"I think strange things happen in careers in the arts," the disembodied Metcalf continued. "That, at a given point in somebody's career, if they have talent at all, and if they hang in for, let's say, forty years or something of this kind, that everybody in magazines and in the publishing trade and in the media all sort of get together, all at the same time, and say, 'okay, now it's time to turn this person into a Grand Old Man.' And articles will start to appear and suddenly somebody who's been not ignored, but who's just been a humdrum member of the literary community for years and years, suddenly becomes a Grand Old Man."

I watched Davies closely as we sat there listening to Metcalf's voice come out of the cassette machine on the table in front of us. Admittedly, it would be hard to read his expression at any time because of the heavy-framed glasses he wore, with one lens blacked out to cover his bad eye, but still, I saw no flicker of anger, resentment, or even surprise.

When the tape ended, I asked for his reaction. He chose to ignore the first part of Metcalf's comments and dealt, instead, with the second part.

"You see, what he talks about is 'forty years,'" Davies responded. "With me it hasn't been forty years, it's been barely ten years. The greatest praise of my work has not come from Canadian critics, most certainly not. I presume John Metcalf — whom I do not know — is a Canadian critic. No, it has come from Scandinavia and it has come from Great Britain and it has come, rather surprisingly to me, from South America. Now I find that my books are suddenly beginning to make an appearance in Israel. This would not happen because the Israelis wanted to sanctify a Canadian writer who'd been writing for forty years. They've only heard about him in the last five years. So I don't pay much attention to that kind of thing."

Davies began lecturing me on how respected Canadian writers and Canadian writing are abroad — which he had also done in our previous meeting.

"It's very hard, I think, for a lot of Canadians to understand that a writer like Alice Munro has something other to say than just stories about small-town Canada. It's a kind of vision of life and an expansion of experience which gets through to these people abroad, who are, if I may say so without being offensive, rather more sophisticated than some of our Canadian critics."

I went back to the Kulyk Keefer review, quoting her calling Davies "Canada's foremost talking head." Given the autograph incident I had witnessed years earlier and magazine cover stories and the like, I wanted to know how he felt about this type of celebrity.

"It is not of my choice," he answered, still polite and courteous but beginning to sound a trifle irritated with my line of questioning. "It is a thing that you have to do nowadays if you are an author. I don't wish to do it, but it is a thing that people are compelled to do. I know that, for instance, all the authors that I know in Canada whose work is widely regarded had to do it. It's just part of the job.

"You see, I have to finish all this dashing around and talking about this book before I can get down to writing a new one," he complained. "Nowadays it's not enough that you should write a book, you have to go around and beat the drum about it. I don't like it, but it's just something that you have to do. And you either behave in a very fancy way and say, 'I'll have nothing to do with that, it is low and vulgar,' or you do it. And if you're a tradesman and a workman, you do it."

I decided to try to end the interview on a lighter note, so I thanked him for putting up with me playing the Metcalf excerpt, then I joked that I could give him Metcalf's address if he wanted to go around and punch him out.

Davies actually smiled and said, "No, no, no, no. Let him say his say, and let those who will, listen."

"Oh, well . . . then we'll get you together for drinks sometime," I suggested.

Now he was laughing outright. "Oh please, no, no, no."

❐

If there is a required reading list for those souls condemned to eternity in hell, Sylvia Fraser's *The Book of Strange: A Journey* will be right up at the top.

Fraser is the author of five novels and, in 1987, her first-person account of incest, *My Father's House*, won the Canadian Authors' Association Award for Non-Fiction. But the 1992 *Book of Strange* transformed her overnight into the Shirley MacLaine of Canada.

Cloaked in the specious phrases often used to describe para-psychological theories, the book's publicity spoke of "first-hand knowledge of telepathy, precognition, meaningful coincidence, psychic healing, multiple personality and intimations of after-life survival."

Among a raft of extraordinary claims, Fraser suggested that the cancer that had killed her sister — and that began around her eye — was the direct result of having witnessed the evil (incest) in the family home when they were both young. Particularly offensive was her suggestion that the proper frame of mind could help cure various lethal diseases, if only people would accept this as fact. As far as I was concerned, this kind of idiotic and dangerous thinking didn't save artist Jack Chambers and it didn't save actor Steve McQueen, just two of its victims.

When Sylvia Fraser came into the studios she was in a bubbly mood. I gathered from her that the book tour had been going well, meaning most interviewers were taking her seriously. I told her before we began that I didn't agree with much, and perhaps all, of what was in the book. She nodded agreeably and said that was fine with her.

We began by talking about coincidence and her belief that even the smallest coincidences are part of some larger web of synchronicity. She had an example: an actress who had portrayed her in a play based on *My Father's House* needed to get her hair done for the performance and picked a hairdresser at random out of the telephone book in Toronto. It turned out to be Fraser's own hairdresser. What did this mean?

"I'm saying that, in terms of the larger context, this seems to indicate that there are force fields that we cannot see that have some kind of influence on our lives," she maintained.

She told stories about the death of her grandmother and of her father that she claimed indicated the existence of telepathy. She talked about the psychic that she visited regularly.

"If you live in a society that denies these experiences," she told me, "you have a choice: you can either deny them too and throw them out and say they didn't happen, or else you can look for a broader framework of reference in which to understand them. As a philosophy student, I already knew of a broader framework of reference and that was that of Plato, Pythagoras, Carl Jung, William James. So I simply began to explore the world of science to see what I could find that corroborated with that other philosophic concept, and I found masses of material that did."

"I don't want to sound too facetious here," I interjected, "but do you think that Jung and Plato and the rest of them that you quote would also believe in healing a cat with the laying on of hands? Because you describe that too, and it's things like that, frankly, that for me takes this over the top. You seem to be willing to believe things that are just nuts."

"I didn't say that I did," she countered.

"But you said you laid your hands on it and the cat was fine when it was over."

"Yes." She seemed flustered. "The subtitle of the book is 'a journey'; it's a quest. I'm asking questions. I'm not giving answers." Her tone was quickly turning frosty. "Let me ask you, Ken, would it have been easier to understand if it was my dying sister that I laid hands on? Was it because it was a cat and you can talk in a trivial way, because it's a cat?"

"I can trivialize it and make a joke out of it," I replied, "because it's a cat, but if it was your sister I wouldn't because it would be a lot more serious. But I wouldn't believe that either."

"But *I* don't necessarily believe it . . . but . . . I think . . . let me . . . ," she was beginning to sputter. "It's a quest . . . and let me talk about western medicine in general . . ." and she went off on another topic.

By the end of the interview Sylvia Fraser's good humour had vanished, and she barely said two words to me as she left the radio station.

❐

Peter Gzowski came around in the fall of 1988 to promote his memoirs. It was the third time I had interviewed him so I knew a couple of things about him: he was very competitive and he was a different guy away from the microphone than the one CBC radio listeners knew as the rambling, warm, and fuzzy radio host of "Morningside."

Gzowski maintained, perhaps a tad disingenuously, that he has always been just a writer working on the radio and is uncomfortable being the person written about, rather than the person doing the writing. We chatted about his tenure at "Morningside," his love of chamber music, and the popularity, or lack of it, for local CBC radio programs. Finally I broached the touchy subject of the real Peter Gzowski.

"The book gives the impression that you're a different person in a lot of respects, off the air than you are on the air," I ventured.

He paused for a second or two. "Um . . . well, yes and no . . ."

"Not Jekyll and Hyde, certainly?"

"No, not Jekyll and Hyde," he answered.

"But you're not a socially gregarious person?"

"I absolutely am not," he responded with apparent honesty. "I really dislike that part of life, the cocktail party, the idle chatter. And I guess having a job that requires me to talk one-on-one for three hours every morning makes me dislike it even more. But, no, I'm not at all a social animal. Another difference — and the one I think you're gently alluding to — is that I'm nicer on the radio than I am in private. And I think probably the older I get, and the nicer I get on the radio, the nastier I get away from it." He was warming to his subject.

"From time to time I say things around the office, or in the presence of my equally irreverent children, and people say, boy, if we had a tape recorder here, we could end your career. Because I make, usually — no, always — always in jest, the most outrageous sexist remarks or racial slurs . . . I'm always sending up that world. But, boy, if you ever wrote them down, whooo, would I ever be dead meat!"

Three months prior to this meeting with Gzowski, I had shared a few heady moments in his company at the National Radio Awards in Toronto. He and I were the only two broadcasters to win two "Nellies" each. The leads of every story from the *Globe and Mail* to *Maclean's* magazine carried both of our names. This was pretty commonplace stuff for him, I suppose, but for me it was like an intense, legal high with no side effects.

Gzowski and I had not seen each other at the awards festivities: the private radio types had a large, alcohol-sodden party afterwards; the CBC people, I guess, just went on home to watch *The National*. Still, I was surprised that he hadn't mentioned it at all during our conversation, not even in our limited chatting before the tape rolled. I raised it jokingly, just to see if there really was a sense of competition. I didn't expect there would be. After all, this guy was the host of a popular national radio program for three hours every day, a virtual folk hero, while I was just the local guy who got lucky.

"So, you want to come down to my office and look at my Nellies?" I ribbed him.

"I have five," he shot back. Then realizing, I think, that he sounded a touch too aggressive, he turned it into a bit of school-yard humour with a "Nyaa, nyaa" taunt and laughed.

I laughed uneasily along with him. When I aired the interview I carefully edited that part out.

12

A Slap
in the Mouth
or a Slug
from a .45

Like many people, I have a secret passion when it comes to books. If left alone, with plenty of free time on my hands and no pressures to read the current politically correct novel, I will indulge myself in . . . detective fiction.

Away back in the early seventies, an old friend of mine handed me a paperback by Rex Stout, called *Fer-de-Lance*. It was a detective novel written in the thirties and it featured an overweight, orchid-growing, gastronomic sleuth by the name of Nero Wolfe. I was hooked from the first chapter.

Being poor at the time, I scoured secondhand bookstores for more and they were easy to find. I discovered that Rex Stout was one of those self-made men who had put together his fortune concocting a bookkeeping process that was used by banks everywhere. Then, in middle age, Stout turned to writing. At the time of his death, some eight or nine years after I discovered him, he had written nearly fifty Nero Wolfe books, all told in the form of notes kept by the detective's faithful right-hand man, the peerless Archie Goodwin.

How can I describe the joy of opening a new Nero Wolfe novel? Or the feeling when Wolfe, a learned man of meticulous habit, ventured outside the cocoon of his 35th Street brownstone in New York City and did something out of character? It was that feeling of wanting to turn to the person next to you — on the train, the bus, in bed at home — and say, hey, listen to this.

I bought and consumed every single book Stout wrote, and dreamed of travelling down to New England to interview him. He died before I was ever in the position to be able to do that.

But that passion prompted me to turn to other forms of the genre, and I found a world that gave me immeasurable pleasure. Writers like Dashiell Hammett, Raymond Chandler, John D. MacDonald, Ross MacDonald, Dorothy Sayers, Agatha Christie (though only the Hercule Poirot books, nothing else), Robert Parker, and, especially, Elmore Leonard.

❐

Being an old blues fan, the very name of Elmore Leonard invoked the image of Elmore James, so I was predisposed to like him before I even read his material. I do remember a slight hesitation when I read a magazine column by the ultraconservative journalist George F. Will, who lauded Leonard's gift of dialogue and referred to him as his friend "Dutch." But I didn't let that stop me and I'm still glad to this day it didn't.

Elmore Leonard is one of those writers who has no pretensions about his craft. He writes the kind of fiction that sells. Having been born and raised in Ottawa, I can still remember the thrill at reading one of his crime novels, set in Detroit (his locales are always Detroit/Windsor, South Florida, Puerto Rico, or New Orleans), and coming across this passage:

> Framed on the wall behind her and almost out of focus was an enlarged printed quotation that read: Whatever women do, they must do twice as well as men to be thought half as good. Luckily this is not difficult — Charlotte Whitton, Mayor of Ottawa, 1963.

Now that, I remember thinking at the time, is research.

In 1991, Elmore Leonard was in Toronto and I arranged to travel there to interview him. We met in the closed restaurant of his hotel, with the sound of the establishment's pet macaw in the background.

Short, bearded, and bespectacled, Elmore Leonard was friendly and unassuming. I liked him instantly.

Leonard's gift, as George Will had rightly pointed out, is his dialogue. He has an ear perfectly pitched to the accents, inflections, and diction of an impressively wide range of characters. I had always assumed this came from his extensive background in movies and television, so I started with questions about that part of his career. To my surprise, he said his first experience in TV was only in the early eighties when he wrote *High Noon, Part Two: The Return of Will Caine,* starring Lee Majors. The show, he laughed, was doomed from the start and he said he only did it for the money.

In fact, while Leonard's books had always received wide critical acclaim, their inevitable translations to the screen were always dismal failures. I asked him about one particularly dreadful effort based on a good Leonard novel called *Stick.* The movie starred Burt Reynolds and bombed after the studio hired another writer to rewrite most of the finished product, then paid Reynolds a truckload of money to reshoot the new scenes.

"I talked to the writer who re-did it," Leonard told me. "And he didn't have a credit. I said, 'your name's not up there,' and he said, 'oh no, it's your story,' and I said, 'no, I'm going to insist that your name is up there too.' I wasn't going to take the entire rap for that thing, see? But you know when you're going to work in Hollywood that these things can happen. So you can't be that surprised. The idea is to take the money and run," he grinned.

I was intrigued by his sense of commerce when he spoke about his writing. He explained that back in the fifties westerns were what sold; men's magazines like Argosy paid five hundred dollars for a short story and a thousand for a long. But when TV appropriated the western at the end of that decade, the pulp magazines disappeared and so did the market. Leonard left full-time writing and became an advertising copywriter in the early sixties. Five years later, he sold the screenplay for his story "Hombre" to Twentieth Century Fox, and it became a movie starring Paul Newman. This bit of good fortune gave him the money to go back to writing. He chose crime fiction.

"The contemporary scene is much more interesting to me because it's so big. A western is a western. I think that if I wrote a western now, I would do it better but it would require an awful lot of work. You're not concerned about the dialogue so much in a western. There's a tradition of western dialogue that has come out of movies, primarily, and that's what you use. But now, writing crime fiction, I don't come out of a tradition. I didn't come out of the Hammett/Chandler school.

"I don't write private eye stories," Leonard continued. "I'll have cops in my stories, but I think only once have I written what you would call a 'procedural,' where the lieutenant of homicide is after somebody. I've avoided the procedural because the guy's only doing his job. He's not personally involved. But in the one I wrote, he becomes personally involved with the bad guy. So, in a sense, it's a western." He laughed. "An eastern western."

That brought our conversation around to the matter of dialogue. Criminals, "low-lifes," cops, lawyers, and the multiplicity of characters who populate the world Elmore Leonard describes in his novels are richly served by his ability to portray them succinctly. I mentioned that I had read Ross MacDonald's Lew Archer books for years before I realized his characters said things like, "I could of done . . . ," when they properly should have been saying, "I could have done . . ."

I asked him if it was this type of written speech pattern — what people actually say instead of what they should say — that makes the dialogue so convincing to the reader. He said he had discussed this very point with fellow crime writer George Higgins and both had agreed it was something they would never do.

"We think it's a cheat," he said. "The person saying 'could of' is not thinking that, he's thinking 'could have.' It's just not right. I usually have them say 'could've.' But I always use 'gonna,' instead of 'going to,' because that's the way I hear it. Most people, and it doesn't matter how educated they are, say 'gonna.' And I usually leave the 'g' on 'ing' words."

I realized as he spoke that he probably could not explain, beyond the technicalities, how he captured that authenticity of conversation. I asked him if he thought that were true.

He agreed immediately, saying it just seemed to be a knack for recognizing the natural flow of talk between people. "I do have one rule, though," he said, as our conversation came to an end. "If it sounds like writing, rewrite it."

❏

If Elmore Leonard didn't come out of the Dashiell Hammett/ Raymond Chandler school of detective fiction, Robert B. Parker certainly did.

Parker is well known for his continuing characters: Spenser, the literate, athletic private eye with no first name, Spenser's psychologist girlfriend, Susan Silverman, and his sleek African-American muscleman pal named Hawk. Spenser has appeared in nearly two dozen books to date; those books are characterized by Parker's lean, Hemingwayesque writing and a gift — like Elmore Leonard — for dialogue.

In a number of the early Spenser books there isn't a lot of action, at least for crime stories. I remember lending a copy of the Spenser novel *Early Autumn* to a friend. When she gave it back a few weeks later I asked if she liked it. She shook her head and said she found it boring. "Nothing happened," she complained.

Parker revelled in literate and hip references in his titles: *The*

Widening Gyre (Yeats), *A Catskill Eagle* (Melville), *Pale Kings and Princes* (Keats), *Mortal Stakes* (Frost), and *Early Autumn* (saxophonist Stan Getz's signature tune).

As the novels gained in popularity, Parker began putting Spenser and Hawk into more and more outlandish situations, predicaments reminiscent of James Bond rather than Philip Marlowe. Even though I was a committed fan of the series, I was starting to question Parker's wisdom and so, I suspect, were many of his readers.

But at the time I met him in 1988 Robert Parker was still at his peak. The Spenser books had been transformed into a television series starring Robert Urich, and Parker, whose doctoral thesis had been on the work of Chandler, Hammett, and Ross MacDonald, was completing Chandler's final unfinished work. *Poodle Springs*, released in 1989, was to be a monumental failure, combining the worst elements of both writers rather than the best. This was not to stop Parker two years later from writing an entirely new Philip Marlowe novel, *Perchance to Dream*, an exercise in self-indulgence for which few forgave him.

My interview with the writer was conducted in a back booth of a fern bar down near the lakefront in Toronto. It was a place popular with editors and publicity types from the various publishing houses in the neighbourhood.

I had seen an interview with him the year before on TVOntario, and had heard him be gruff and testy in an interview with Peter Gzowski on CBC radio, but I was still taken aback by the large, florid, and self-confident-to-the-point-of-arrogant person I met. As we positioned ourselves in the booth I noted his size, trying not to stare at the gold chain around his neck that threatened to disappear in the folds. As he told me himself, he bore a striking resemblance to NFL player Dick Butkis.

Probably everybody — interviewers included — has some story about being disappointed with the behaviour of some notable they admired. I remember a friend telling me about attending a conference in the United States at which the novelist Richard Ford was speaking. Later, as my friend was leaving his hotel, he saw Ford standing near the curb waiting for his car. He went over just as the car pulled up, politely introduced himself, and told Ford how much he admired Ford's novels. Ford — renowned for his abilities to capture the delicate sensibilities of human relationships — looked at my friend, said, "Fuck off," turned, climbed into his car, and drove off.

My experience with Robert Parker was certainly nothing like that but it did leave me with a sense of disappointment, though to this day I'm still not sure why.

I told him that I had always thought his Spenser character was the natural offspring of Ross MacDonald's Lew Archer, rather than Raymond Chandler's Philip Marlowe. This, I said boldly, was because the theme of the past coming back to touch lives in the present — a common thread in most of the Archer novels — was often the plot focus of Spenser books. Parker raised his eyebrows and told me with some distaste that MacDonald lacked "energy," though he was more responsible than either Raymond Chandler or Dashiell Hammett for making the hard-boiled detective novel accepted by the public.

"I'm going to speak at Yale next month," he told me. "I think without Ross MacDonald that never would have happened."

I wanted to know if, at the start of his writing career, he was intimidated by the critical praise associating him with the Chandler/Hammett legacy — if he thought he had to uphold a certain tradition.

"What worked in the early days was to identify the kinds of books that I wrote," he answered. "I am a writer who is like Hammett and Chandler as opposed to a writer who is like Agatha Christie. It was a kind of shorthand to say this was a book that had characteristics that seemed Chandleresque as opposed to characteristics that were like Willa Cather or something. To that end it was useful to me. But my mind just doesn't work in that way in terms of whether I will get better or worse, or have any-body to climb over, or am intimidated by the comparison. I do the best I can with a book, then I send it off, and I start another one and I do the best I can with that one. I try quite actively not to read what anyone writes about me or what television says about me — I just work away at it. I think the effect it had in the early days was salutary in that it helped me a lot career-wise.

"I think there are two areas a writer deals in," he continued. "One, how well he is doing as an artist, or if he's an artist at all. And the other area is how much money is he making? The Hammett/Chandler comparisons helped me in the money-making area but had no effect in the area of art."

We talked about the lack of interest the Spenser books gener-ated in Great Britain and the intense interest they created in Japan and why that might be. Then I decided to broach the subject of the criticism of his most recent work at that time, *A Catskill Eagle*. The novel had been savaged by critics who said Spenser had become a James-Bondian superhero and the violence had esca-lated proportionately.

"I got a lot of criticism — starting with the publisher before it was published," he admitted. "The publisher wanted some changes made that I wouldn't make and they said if I didn't make them the critics would jump on me. And I said, 'yeah, but the book needs them, I think they belong in the story.' And I think we were both right. I think what I did was appropriate to the story and the critics jumped on it.

"It was a bigger book, considerably bigger than the others, and it was an attempt at some things — there's nothing more unseemly than a writer explaining what you should have understood in his book and I don't plan to do that —" he interrupted himself "— having to do with myth and heroism.

"The interesting thing about all of that is that in the United States when it first came out, *Time* magazine said it was the best book I'd ever written and *Newsweek* said it was the worst."

Hawk, the weight-lifting, flashy-dressing, champagne-sipping, shaven-headed black hoodlum-with-a-moral-code, has attracted his own fans. Parker had said that white people were really taken with Hawk and I asked him why.

"I'm not quite sure," he replied. He said he had gotten some feedback from blacks on the character and all of it was positive. He said a professor of literature had described Hawk as the only black in contemporary American writing who was autonomous, not somebody's sidekick: a man with an identity of his own.

"People love Hawk," Parker elaborated. "They want more of him; they don't like books in which he's not featured enough. If I had to guess, and it's only a guess, probably what's comforting to a white audience is the bond between the black man and the white man as opposed to the real world in which there's a great deal of animosity between blacks and whites, particularly in Boston where the books are set.

"There's also some myth working in there. There's a theory about American literature to which I subscribe, most prominently presented by a critic named Leslie Fiedler, that the American myth is a black man and a white man in a kind of wilderness situation whose commitment to each other is irrevocable. He points to Ishmael and Queequeg, Huck and Jim on the raft, and in 'low' culture to the Lone Ranger and Tonto. If he's right, then it should work that way and people should respond not so much to Hawk as to the relationship between the two of them. But whatever, it's nice to see an integrated society, no matter how small, that works."

❐

If there is an opposite to Robert Parker in all respects it is Dick Francis. Where Parker is tall, broad, and red-faced, sporting that tight gold chain around his substantial neck framed by an open-collared sports shirt, Francis is small (as befits a former jockey), compact, and tastefully dressed in jacket, white shirt, and tie. Where the Spenser novels feature a continuing cast of characters enmeshed in new situations, the thirty-odd Francis books feature the same characters with different names involved in stories set in and around racetracks.

Dick Francis is a remarkably civil man. On the two occasions I have met him, I have been amazed at how graciously he takes the book-tour business, considering, with thirty-one novels under his belt and worldwide success, he certainly doesn't need to do it.

After retiring as a jockey in Great Britain and writing his auto-biography, *The Sport of Queens*, Francis turned to crime novels. His first novel, *Dead Cert*, went straight to number one.

Living now in Florida most of the year, his writing schedule never varies. He begins each book in January and finishes in mid-May. His publisher comes over from England, stays a couple of days discussing the book, leaves on a Friday night, and the book goes to the typesetter on Monday morning. Two weeks later the proofs are sent over to Francis for correcting, sent back for print-ing, and the book is released in September.

During the actual writing of each book — books that he said are "the same, but different" — his daily schedule is also precise. He gets up at six thirty each morning, does his ablutions, drinks a glass of orange juice, watches *Good Morning, America* or *The Today Show* for a bit, walks along the beach until seven thirty, swims in the ocean, then in his pool, and sits down at around a quarter to nine and starts thinking about what he will write that day. He told me it is usually ten o'clock before he gets anything down on paper. Then he writes for two hours, breaks for lunch, and writes for another two hours in the afternoon. He only takes days off when there is an interesting horse race on. He also told me he writes everything in longhand in a series of notebooks, then transfers it all to his computer.

What I found so fascinating about Francis's approach was his apparent lack of the uncertainty that plagues most other writers:

Dick Francis appeared totally at ease with everything he writes.

I asked him if he read his dialogue out loud, as many writers do, to make sure it sounded like real speech.

"No, I don't read it out loud," he said. "But I do like to have the words flowing. I hope you'll find that I use very few superfluous sentences or words and I like every word to count. If a sentence doesn't flow, I rub it out. But once it's down, I do one draft and that's all that happens. Once it's down, it stays."

"So you're not a big rewrite man?" I asked.

"No. I don't rewrite at all. Just the odd word."

Most writers would cringe hearing this, but it's just as well Francis doesn't spend a lot of time rewriting; his publisher has demanded a new novel each and every year. Once, in 1965, his publisher wanted two novels, one for the spring and the second for the Christmas trade.

This may sound crass, but Dick Francis has never made any pretence of writing great literature. His initial decision to write crime novels, he said, came after a few years in journalism and the financial pressures of two college-age boys and a mortgage.

"I used to read a lot of fiction when I was travelling around on trains," he told me. "And also, standing around the railroad station, I would see people reading books and buying them and whatnot and I would keep an eye on them. I'm a little bit commercially minded, and it was the adventure story and mysteries that were the ones they seemed to like. So I thought, I'll get into that field."

He admitted that after more than thirty books he occasionally discovers he is plagiarizing himself by repeating passages from earlier stories. He said the joy of the writing for him was learning about other disciplines, like pharmacology or diplomacy or veterinary medicine.

Dick Francis was seventy-two when I last met him and I asked him if the day would come when he would just call it quits and retire permanently in Florida.

"Well, I suppose there will come a day when I can't do it," he mused, more to himself than to me. "But I'm committed already to four more so I'll have to go on to age seventy-six at least." Then he laughed. "How long after that I don't know. I said to my publisher's wife about sixteen years ago, 'if I write a book that hasn't got horses or racing in it, will you still publish it?' Because I thought I might go into another field. And she said, 'yes, we'll publish anything you write.'"

He paused.

"Then she said, 'we'd rather you didn't do so, though.'"

13

Mordecai
Now
and Then

Mordecai Richler is scarier than Margaret Atwood. Where Atwood makes you feel like the butt of some cosmic joke that you can never hope to understand, Richler, with one heavy sigh and a raised eyebrow, can dismiss you and your annoying questions for all eternity.

I first spoke with him in the mid-eighties when his collection of essays, *Home Sweet Home*, was published. It was late in the afternoon when I arrived, tape machine in hand, at the door to his suite in the Chateau Laurier in Ottawa. I was a bit nervous, having admired *The Apprenticeship of Duddy Kravitz* and *St. Urbain's Horsemen*, and knowing that he had a reputation for being irascible. Richler caught me a bit off guard by appearing behind me in the hall as I knocked on his door, carrying a brandy snifter in one hand and a small, black cheroot in the other. He brushed past me into the suite, muttering about a dinner appointment that evening.

With his sad, hound-dog face, unkempt dark hair, and rumpled appearance, Richler reminded me of a towel discarded on the bathroom floor.

I set up my tape machine on a small table to the side of the two large wing chairs from which we faced each other. We began the interview, Richler with the snifter in one hand, the cheroot in the other, waving it in the air as he spoke. He used his deep voice to great effect, particularly when he paused to think about his next words.

We were about fifteen minutes into our conversation, Richler speaking quite freely, when I glanced over at the recorder. The needle on the VU meter was bouncing happily back and forth to the cadence of our voices but, to my horror, I realized the cassette tape inside the machine was not moving. In fact, it appeared not to have moved at all. Nothing of what Richler had said to me had been recorded. In my nervousness I had hit the record button without realizing the pause button was also engaged. I reached over as unobtrusively as I could and released it.

Now that I was finally recording, I was faced with a dilemma: did I admit to Richler what I had done, looking like a rank amateur and risking his contempt? Did I try to ask my first few questions again, cleverly rephrasing them to elicit similar and maybe even better answers? Or did I just choose to forget the whole fifteen minutes and carry on with other questions, hoping to get enough for an actual interview?

My fear of Richler won out and I chose the last. Thankfully Richler was feeling verbose that day and he spoke for another half hour.

Over the next couple of years, I saw Richler at various political events — leadership conventions and the like — hanging out with Allan Fotheringham and Marjorie Nichols, schlepping around in a baggy raincoat looking eerily like Peter Falk in *Columbo*.

It wasn't until the fall of 1989 that I had a chance to meet him again. His novel *Solomon Gursky Was Here* had just been published and he was passing through Ottawa.

We met one morning at the back of the closed coffee shop in his hotel, him with a coffee, cheroot, and no cognac this time — though he said he would dearly like one. I made sure my tape machine was recording.

Solomon Gursky Was Here was Richler's first novel in eight years since *Joshua Then and Now*. It was a sprawling book that traced the history of the Gursky brothers, who — Bronfman-like — built a distillery empire out of their rum-running operations during Prohibition.

Richler said he only put pen to paper after he had read everything he could about the Franklin Expedition, which made up the historical passages of the book.

"I began to go through various drafts of these chapters," he told me, "and to begin with, the research stuck out because you become a prisoner of your research; you want to use all of it. So it was a question of thinning it out and thinning it out, making it more economical and making it my own. That was something I wasn't used to doing. The situations I know are voices I've heard, so there were certain risks and difficulties involved, but I enjoyed doing it."

Trapped by his research? This was a pitfall for new writers, but surely a seasoned novelist like himself could avoid it?

"It suffered from too many facts to begin with," he answered. "I went to libraries and learned about what life was like on the ships, and what the sailors did and what they ate, what their sleeping circumstances were, and so on. Then I began to put all of this in and, of course, I wasn't writing a novel about the Franklin Expedition, so it was unnecessary. And what happened is that in certain sections the novel came to a stop.

"So I began to chop and cut and there was a certain amount of blood on the floor, but there always is."

"At one point in the book," I said, "you have Solomon Gursky say: 'Gerald Murphy had it wrong, living two, maybe three times is the best revenge.' That's one of the nubs of the book, right?"

He actually smiled at me. "That *is* the nub of the book," he answered. "The original saying was 'living well is the best revenge,' but the spur, the notion behind the novel, nebulous as it was, was to write about a man who was not content to live within the confines of one life — which all of us are doomed to do — and was a sufficient trickster, or magician, to invent other lives for himself. And that was what got me started many years ago."

We talked about the various obsessions evident in the novel ("it's a book about obsessions on many levels"), and about the several father/son relationships that also appear. Then I quoted *Toronto Star* book critic Philip Marchand, who wrote that he could hear Richler reciting Faulkner about disliking both Jews and Gentiles, as Richler decimated the two groups in *Solomon Gursky*.

"He heard me tell that story once about Faulkner, I'm sure," Richler responded. "That's why he brought it up.

"You know, I'm a satirist. This is a novel of character but there are long satirical stretches, and it's a comic novel really, something some people might not understand. I was amazed to read some of the reviews — you'd think you were in for a very heavy time," he said, sipping his coffee. "This really is a comic novel.

"Mr. Bernard [one of the novel's more eccentric characters] is in many ways an engaging man. He's a scoundrel and a ruffian, but a man who, on his deathbed, can say 'if God exists, I'm fucked.' He has a certain amount of self-awareness. I mean, you can't really hate a man who can come up with that."

That same character in the novel expressed the desire to have his biography written but "I don't want a Canadian, I want the best."

"That's representative of the feeling here," Richler remarked, "that a Canadian can't be the best. That's something we all suffer from, which is totally unfair and not the case, but I'm sure it's the general attitude."

I told him that author Leon Rooke had done many different versions of his novel *The Good Baby* before he settled on the one that was finally published. I asked Richler if he had done something similar with *Solomon Gursky*.

"I began this novel, I guess about ten or twelve years ago," he said. "And I would get up to a certain point, couldn't go any further, and would go back and start rewriting. I would try to climb in a basement window, as it were. Then I'd get up to that point again and I just couldn't go any further. So I put it aside, wrote *Joshua Then and Now* and did a number of other things, then about five years ago I took it all out and sat down, and I've been working on it, to the exclusion of anything else for the most part, for this last five years.

"The novel," he went on, "before I finally hit on this structure, had very many different structures. For a long time it began with Mr. Bernard's birthday party, but then Ephraim loomed far more important and I decided it was much more important to begin with him."

By now Richler was on his third or fourth coffee refill and was behaving as if my presence was actually tolerable. I asked him about the complexity of this novel — with its plots and subplots, shifts from generation to generation, and large cast of characters. Was he concerned that many readers might find it too much work?

"Yes, it was a concern of mine and it does take a certain amount of work," he replied, with a chuckle. "And there's very little I can do about it.

"But the danger is that when you are writing it, and spending all of these years, you know everything so intimately, so it's all clear to you. For the reader, coming to it fresh, there might be certain difficulties getting into it but then I think once you get into it, it does run."

My next meeting with Richler came in 1992 in the middle of a storm of controversy centred around his political opinions. His latest book, *Oh Canada, Oh Quebec*, a portion of which had been excerpted months earlier in *The New Yorker* magazine, had touched off a rage of resentment in his home province.

He had done a raft of interviews in the autumn and then, when the whole book was published, another round in the spring. By the time he came to Ottawa, he was no longer interested in talking about it and had only come because of a commitment to read from the book at the National Library.

For me, it was another interview in another hotel coffee shop. We sat amid the clinking coffee cups and breakfast conversations of other hotel guests.

I decided that Richler would likely be so annoyed at having to answer the same questions all over again that I needed a different approach. My friend Joe Cummings, a sports broadcaster, told me that Richler was a huge baseball fan and, in particular, an aficionado of the old Montreal Royals. This was the very same team, Joe told me, that Chuck Connors — TV's *The Rifleman* — once played on.

Armed with this flimsy bit of sports trivia and a nearly absolute vacuum of knowledge or interest in the game itself, I foolishly decided to use baseball as my opening into the Richler interview.

I knew Richler had attended the Expos home opener the previous day at Olympic Stadium in Montreal, so I started with that.

"Somebody told me this morning that you're a big Montreal Royals fan and that this was the team Chuck Connors used to play for. Is that true?" I asked.

He broke into a smile. "He did, yes. But I was gone by that time. I used to go to the Montreal Royals games; we had a splendid team. Won the Little World Series several times — it was the Dodgers's number one farm team and I dare say a better team —" he laughed, "— than the Expos. There were some wonderful players there.

"They drew big crowds, you know," he went on, apparently not even needing me to ask any more questions, which was fine with me since I had none to ask. "And a very big francophone crowd. During Little World Series, they'd rope off centre field, put in another couple of thousand seats, so you'd get about twenty-three, twenty-four thousand people there. During the war, we had a couple of interesting French-Canadian players off the sandlots."

I expressed amazement at the size of the crowds and suggested that those numbers would be considered very respectable even by today's standards, particularly for the Expos in 1991–92.

Richler laughed again. "The Expos would be grateful, yes. It's a pity about the Expos. There've been several good teams and Charles Bronfman certainly put his heart into it — and his money. The city became disenchanted with the team. I think after Rick Monday hit that home run, which knocked us out of World Series contention, the romance was over."

Despite having witnessed it on television with George Jonas, I was still only vaguely aware of the now-legendary homer that Monday hit in 1981 that cost the Expos the National League East pennant. Its significance to Montrealers wouldn't become real to me until the summer after this interview when I stood with a friend in the Baseball Hall of Fame in Cooperstown, New York, and listened to Rick Monday tell us how it was only recently that the threats on his life had stopped.

So it was with genuine innocence that I asked Richler if that homer was really the turning point in the Expos relationship with their fans.

"I think so . . . ," he said, looking at me for the first time as it started to dawn on him that I was totally out of my depth with this topic. "There were too many disappointed people."

Time to bail out, I thought.

"Let's see if I can somehow segue that into the subject we're supposed to be talking about," I said to him.

"Oh, I'd much rather talk about baseball."

"I know you would . . . but how's this? Has there been a role played in Quebec by baseball in bringing the two cultures together?"

He brightened instantly.

"Oh yes, there were teams in Quebec City and in Sherbrooke. There were French-Canadian players — not many of them made it to the majors but not many English players made it to the majors, either.

"So, yeah, it was a sport that appealed to francophones, unlike football which doesn't appeal to francophones, or to me for that matter."

As I began moving into the area of the controversy surrounding the book, I decided to try to continue the male-bonding, sports bonhomie in the hopes of keeping Richler loose and free-wheeling with his answers.

"You've pissed off just about everybody with this book, haven't you," I joked, figuring he would respond in kind. I should have known better.

"Well, maybe you're not sufficiently widely read," he suggested, giving me a withering glance. "Pierre Berton came out with a resounding defence of the book in the *Toronto Star*, Robertson Davies came out in favour of the book and said how funny it was. So, I'm in pretty good company, I think, and there have been a number of very favourable reviews."

"Let me ask you about that," I said, seeing a chance to recover my balance as the interviewer. "As I was reading this book I kept thinking that maybe it was just me who found it funny. Everything I had read about it in advance had indicated it was this heavy-handed tract about the volatile relationship between French and English."

"Yeah, people were pretty fast off the mark. I mean, most of them had not read the book, which is a help," he laughed. "But I consider the book far from ill-tempered. I think it's very fair and funny, because it is a ludicrous situation we are in, it's not a tragic situation."

One of the elements of the controversy was an open letter that had been printed in several newspapers, signed by some prominent Canadians, all disassociating themselves with the book and with Richler. He had not been the only one to point out that the list of names bore a striking similarity to the names that appeared on the board of *Canadian Forum* magazine.

I asked him how he felt about the letter.

He chuckled. "I'm astonished that they would have thought I

wanted to associate with them in any event. Those are just knee-jerk nationalists who have been quarrelling with me for years and I would have considered it embarrassing if they had come out in favour of the book. I just think they're a bunch of fools."

Richler expressed bewilderment over the reaction his book generated in Quebec, saying he had written a long piece twelve years earlier in *Atlantic Monthly* making fun of the same things and nobody reacted at all.

"French nationalists tend to vastly overestimate my influence," he said. "Which I suppose is flattering, but it's kind of silly. It's one man's opinion.

"I think, possibly, Quebeckers, like English Canadians, are very sensitive to being held up to ridicule abroad. But the language law is ridiculous and very funny, and all I did was chronicle the events that led up to it."

As our conversation drew to a close, Richler engaged in a bit of prophesying.

"I think the majority of Quebeckers are very sensible people," he told me. "We're not going to have a separate and sovereign Quebec, but Quebec will continue to prosper within Canada.

"I'm just back from London and Paris where there is sunlight and flowers blossoming everywhere and I think, why am I back here in the middle of this childish quarrel? But I would not live anywhere else in Canada, but in Quebec."

14

New
Voices
in the Choir

L eonard Cohen thinks of himself as a singer rather than a poet and, despite the limitations of his vocal chords, is willing to "take his place in the choir."

There have been plenty of new members to that choir since Cohen joined, and, happily, many of them are Canadian just like Cohen. In this chapter are several of those young singers, some carrying on a tradition, some blazing a new path, and some putting a fresh spin on an old form.

❏

Sarah McLachlan was on the telephone from the Lord Elgin Hotel. She was scheduled to be in my studio for an interview, then make it a few blocks over to the club where she was performing that evening for a live interview on the afternoon drive home show on CBC radio. Her manager had her call me to arrange transportation and that transportation was going to be me and my Subaru station wagon. I told her I would pick her up in the lobby and, to make it easier, I said I would be the one with the dark beard and the Panama hat. To her credit — and this probably endeared her to me for all time — she did not assume that I would know what she looked like and proceeded to give me a description. An hour later, as we worked our way through rush-hour traffic back to the radio station, she asked me who we were listening to on the car's tape machine.

"Van Morrison," I replied, a bit startled.

"I thought so. I've never heard him, but I'm told he's very good."

This was a perplexing revelation. One of the reasons I liked Sarah McLachlan's music was that I heard in it many of the same elements that appear in Van Morrison's music after about 1980. Her new album at the time, *Drawn to the Rhythm*, was a wonderful amalgam of raw emotion, appealing lyrics, haunting vocals, and skilled instrumentation. So it was even more startling to realize how young she was, which, naturally, carried with it the corollary of making me aware of how old I was. I compounded this feeling once we were settled in the studio by telling her that her vocals reminded me of Joan Baez's first album from 1962. She hit me with the first of many dazzling smiles.

"I own it on vinyl too," she said.

"So where do your vocal styles come from?"

"It's funny you would ask," she replied. "The very first people I ever listened to were Joan Baez and Cat Stevens." She paused for a single beat. "I was three or four years old." She burst into laughter. "My mother was really into them, and I was singing all the time, so I picked up on them immediately and learned all the songs and sang them all. So that was when I got a ukulele, when I was four, so I could accompany myself."

McLachlan said she turned to classical guitar around the age of nine or ten and spent most of her time struggling to practise in a house that had one brother upstairs playing heavy metal and the other brother downstairs playing punk. She pursued classical guitar training so she could learn chord structures. This, she believed, would give her the expertise to do what she really wanted to do — sing. Her persistence paid off at the tender age of seventeen.

"I was playing in a band called The October Game," she told

me. "It was the first gig we had ever done together as a band . . . my first band experience outside of classical recitals, which were always miserable. We were opening up for Moev, which is a Nettwerk act, and the guy who is now the head of A&R [Artists and Repertoire] for Nettwerk was the guitar player in that band at the time. He heard me sing and wanted me to come out to Vancouver and do some demos with Moev. Well, I was seventeen and my parents freaked out . . ."

"Yes," I muttered, feeling more like a parent every minute.

". . . I was barely getting through high school at that point, didn't care at all, and they said no way. I was pretty angry about that, but I'm glad they made me hold out because two years later the president of Nettwerk came back to Halifax and offered me a five-record contract out of the blue."

Showing remarkable maturity, McLachlan said she was a bit sceptical about the offer since she had never written a single song and the deal would allow her to write her own material. "I thought about it for three months first. I debated, back and forth, about whether I should do it. I mean, I *really, really, really* wanted to do it but there were a lot of things to weigh out in my own mind. I wanted to finish art college too, but art college was going to be there and this was not going to be there, if I didn't take it. So I figured, *just go for it!* I told my dad — I sat him down and I said, 'listen, I'm not going back to school, this is what I've been offered.' I was terrified to tell my parents. I thought they were just going to hate me. And my dad just sat there and listened and then at the end he said, 'well, we better get you a lawyer.' And I was so happy, because he was so cool about it."

McLachlan approached her Vancouver experience with the same characteristic clearheadedness. She knew she was going to need plenty of help and the people at Nettwerk gave it. "I had no idea where to start and these guys pushed me into formulating patterns. I'd have three or four chords and they'd say, *'okay,* there's a verse, now let's write a chorus.'" She put on a valley-girl cadence.

"'Oh, okay' . . . and so I'd find a couple of other chords . . . I could do it, I could write the song, it's just that I needed somebody to prod me and say, 'stop putting ten chords in — you can do it in three or four.' Editing — they were really editors." (In early 1995, the coproducer and the engineer on McLachlan's debut album launched lawsuits claiming they had cowritten songs that had been credited only to her.)

When it came to writing lyrics, McLachlan managed to stop me in my tracks one more time. I asked if that part, at least, had come easy. "No, not at all," she answered, with that smile. "I'd never written any poetry before or anything like that, either. So I didn't have anything to say, I didn't think. I'd lived a sheltered life in Halifax and hadn't yet learned to step outside myself and be objective about anything that I'd done, or to learn from any experiences. So I just, basically, looked to poetry, looked to creating imagery with words and mood and beautiful sounding things, without really meaning a hell of a lot."

❒

The only thing Holly Cole had in common with Sarah McLachlan was Joan Baez. Sarah McLachlan listened to Baez when she was a kid; Holly Cole appeared to have ironed her hair the same way Baez was rumoured to. That's it for a connection.

I interviewed Holly Cole between her first album, *Girl Talk*, and the release of her second, *Blame It on My Youth*. She was just about to leave for a tour of Japan, which would be staggeringly successful.

Being a new convert to jazz — the Kerouac experience in Quebec City in 1987 had turned me around — I was intrigued by some of the things she had done on *Girl Talk*. The album had been recorded using only one microphone — in the manner of Billy Holiday, though Holiday did it out of necessity, Cole for style. Cole, her piano accompanist Aaron Davis, and upright bass player David Piltch seemed to have captured a certain neo-jazz sensibility, though time and a better appreciation of the genre would alter my belief in that. (A few months after my encounter with Cole, I would spend a sodden afternoon in a bar with photographer John Reeves, who had just completed a book with jazz writer Gene Lees called *Jazz Lives*, and novelist Barry Callaghan, who has nurtured a reputation involving racetracks, booze, literature, booze, blues, booze and jazz and booze. Both were dismissive of Holly Cole and her efforts.)

But none of this had happened when Holly Cole and I sat down in the studio for some girl/boy talk. We spent the first few minutes discussing the technical production of the first record: that it was trial and error when it came to mike placement and that it only took three days — which made the record company very happy.

Cole has a rich voice, evident from her singing, a warm and friendly personality, and the coolest bebop/beat-chick look I have seen in some time. I pulled out a quote from jazz writer Daniel Okrent about "girl" singers (a term that used to be interchangeable with "thrush," "canary," and "chanteuse"). Okrent had written the five requirements for that position: an ability to sing ballads and up-tempo numbers; an evocation of a swaying hemline; display of a sense of humour in phrasing; mastery of a repertoire that doesn't stray into Lloyd Webber; and the ability to flirt with the listener.

Cole seemed discomfited by the list, likely because it reeked of sexism, but agreed that humour was an essential. "Humour is a big part of the show. The challenge, when recording, is to translate that to a recorded product. When you're playing live, people can see your gestures. I do a lot of talking in the show and there's a lot of communication within the band that employs humour and that's hard to translate to a record. Sometimes you don't even know if you want to, because there are certain things that happen live that you wouldn't want on a record anyway. You want them

to be there and gone, good when they're there but still not something you would want to listen to every time you heard that tune."

One of the surprising tracks on *Girl Talk* was the Hank
Williams classic "I'm So Lonesome I Could Cry," done as a slow,
smoky jazz tune. Cole said it came from her eclectic musical background in the Maritimes. "That song in particular was taught to
me by my grandfather," she replied. "I grew up in the Maritimes,
which has a lot of people who are really into country music. In
the Maritimes there isn't a lot of black music listened to at all. I
wasn't introduced to black music until I was sixteen, and that's
when I went to visit my brother who was studying jazz. Now a lot
of my favourite styles of music, like jazz, like funk and soul, are
black styles of music. But I also like some of the white styles of
music, like country, like classical."

The success of that first record came as a pleasant surprise to
Cole, who told me she was so "inside the project" that she really
had no thoughts on how it would be received. Nor, she said, did
she feel any undue pressures about which direction to take with
the second record. "The way I make the choice is I'm dictated by
the music that I want to play. You can be dictated by how successful you want to be, you can try and read the market and do
what they want you to do, if that's what your aim is. But that's
never been *my* aim with the music, or any of us in the band — it's
always been doing the music we want to do. And if other people
like it, it's wonderful for us."

At the time of our interview, Cole had just closed a deal with Blue
Note ("when they talked to us about signing, I was just floored!"),
which ensured distribution of the second album in the United
States, Japan, Australia, Great Britain, and Europe. She said *Blame It
on My Youth* was a "darker" album, with more "obscure" standards
on it, plus one never-before-recorded song by Tom Waits.

"I contacted Tom Waits — aiming high — and asked him if
he'd like to produce our record," she said.

"You mean he has a phone?" I was amazed.

"Yeah," she laughed, "he's a regular guy, it turns out. I couldn't believe it. He said, 'I don't actually produce but I'll put you through to my producer.' So he contacted Greg Cohen, who just loved the first record, so we went and met him and we hit it off and it worked out. I told Greg that I would love it if we could have a Tom Waits song. He gave us some songs that were already recorded by Tom, and I said they were good but not quite right. So Greg phoned Tom and he came up with this new song, 'Purple Avenue.' It was exciting for me because Tom Waits is one of my all-time favourite composers, old or new.

"Although I love his music," she continued, " it's very *male* — most of the songs are from a male perspective. And there were lyrics in this song that I couldn't sing. It was talking about leaving this woman, and there was a lyric about counting the whiskers in the sink. So I had to ask him to change the lyrics and the last thing I wanted to do was call Tom Waits and ask him to change some lyrics. But he actually phoned the studio while we were recording and Greg answered, and Greg was relaying messages from me to Tom and Tom to me, and finally Tom said, 'why don't you just let me talk to her?' So I said —" she dropped her voice to a whisper — "'uh, hello?' I told him that I couldn't sing the lyrics from a woman's point of view, and he said, 'oh yeah, I never thought of that.' So we worked on them, and I had my experience interacting with Tom Waits."

Despite criticism from jazz purists, Holly Cole has gone on to remarkable popularity. When we spoke, her take on the vagaries of success was characteristically down to earth. "This band had been together for five years before the first record came out, so it wasn't like a big producer came by and said, 'Okay, here's a singer and I'm going to find you a band, and we're going to put out a record.' We were a very established band in our own circuit — it was a pretty underground circuit in Toronto — I just thought, 'we're making a record, that's great and let's release it and hope that people buy it.' And they did."

❐

The phrase "Capitalism is killing music" appeared under the title of Billy Bragg's 1988 album, *Workers Playtime*, which, in turn, appeared under one of those highly idealized, Great Leap Forward, Mao-inspired Chinese workers paintings. What he lacks in subtlety, Bragg makes up for in conviction.

I had known of Bragg's existence for some time but had not gone out of my way to listen to his material. The teenaged daughter of my oldest friend, a girl who had lived for several years in Botswana and had been politicized early on, was, my friend told me, completely taken with his music. I decided to give him an ear and I confess to being stunned that anyone this political could muster any kind of loyal audience in the egocentric, greedhead 1980s.

I interviewed Billy Bragg in a studio at a campus radio station after a sold-out concert. He was a slender and pale young man, reminiscent of Sean Penn with a cockney accent. He also had a sense of humour and, to my surprise, a clear vision of where he fit into the lineage of protest singers. "I feel part of a tradition that not only is the obvious one that you'd think of, like the Woody Guthries and the Bob Dylans, but also encapsulates people like Hank Williams, who I class as proto-punk rock: really out there, raw, at the edge, primal rock and roll. A lot of those early rock and rollers came from the same sort of background as Hank came from. So I see a continuation, not only from those long-back days, but also a lot of recent influences. I don't like any comparisons, but the only one I will accept is Phil Ochs, if he'd have seen The Clash when he was nineteen years old."

He took a quick breath. "See, that's the difference. I copped all that influence of Simon and Garfunkel, Dylan, and all that early stuff, but I went through the cleansing fire of punk rock in my formative years. It was happening there in London and it kind of like put a different angle on the way I decided to make music."

I was intrigued by Bragg's identification with Phil Ochs. Not many people still mentioned the troubled protest singer who could write a powerful, defiant, and optimistic song like "I Ain't Marching Anymore" and still be capable of suicide, allegedly over a slight from Dylan. In the final part of his life, Ochs seemed overwhelmed with disillusionment, something that Bragg attributed to the defeat the New Left suffered at the hands of the Chicago Police during the riots at the Democratic National Convention in 1968. Bragg maintained the British Left had a stronger foundation that let it weather these setbacks.

"Well, I think Phil and his generation, who were in that thing — whatever it was — in the sixties that culminated in Chicago in sixty-eight, really I think that was an incredible knockback from which they never really recovered. They'd never experienced anything like that before, so they'd never experienced the knockbacks that occur when you try and go up against authority and the establishment. Whereas, in Britain, in the Socialist tradition, we have a much longer cultural underpinning to what we're trying to do. And there have been more defeats, I must be honest, than victories in our attempts to change the country from a selfish society to a caring society. In our struggles to do that, we've had our fights. So, in Britain, we're more able to deal with that and see it in a longer-term thing."

Bragg wasn't bothered by the fact that the bulk of his audience seemed to be made up of middle-class kids who had no real first-hand experience of the kinds of subjects he turned into song. "Phil Ochs was, to all extents and purposes, a middle-class, North American kid; Bob Dylan was a middle-class, North American kid; Abby Hoffman was definitely; Jerry Rubin has grown up to be a New Age, upper-class kid. So I'm not surprised by that at all. Obviously, people feel that there's something they want from popular culture, other than just buying and selling records, running everything like a corporation, as if it's just ear candy. I'm not decrying people who want to listen to that sort of music — it's up to them — but I think there's more and more young people look-ing for something else, some resonance. Which is why in some ways the media is still obsessed with the sixties; because there was something life-affirming about getting together and trying to work for a common purpose which was fundamentally, you felt anyway, morally above what was going down at the time."

Bragg also made a distinction between young people in Canada and their counterparts in the United States. "I think young people in Canada have more of an idea of the socialist tradition, but in the United States of America I think they have totally lost touch with their socialist tradition because Senator Joe McCarthy encouraged, in the post-war years, the establishment in the United States to rewrite their history in exactly the same way that Joseph Stalin encouraged the Soviet Union to rewrite their history."

As I sat there, slack-jawed and reeling in front of this political rant, Bragg delivered the coup de grace. "You in Canada haven't, and I think the existence of the NDP proves that you haven't. There is a democratic socialist party, similar to the Labour Party in England, that still manages to maybe not get a majority, but at least go rounds with the major parties."

Bragg's manager inserted himself into the conversation, reminding the singer that they had to hit the road in the bus to drive over-night to the next gig. Bragg and I shook hands and parted company. As I made my way back to my car, I remember feeling a touch guilty about having let my political convictions fade over the years. I had been gently chastened by this young man a generation or more behind me. Still, I thought, Billy Bragg is also able to sing one of the loveliest versions of the Left Banke's "Walk Away, Renée" I had ever heard. And there's nothing wrong with that either.

❐

No pictures. The word had come downstairs at the hotel that Daniel Lanois hadn't showered yet, or shaved, and would rather not have his picture taken. I was there to interview him in January of 1990 both for "Medium Rare" and for a magazine called *Metro*, which I edited for a few months. I reluctantly sent the photographer on his way, puzzled because a half hour earlier in the hotel coffee shop I had seen Lanois and another band member eating breakfast.

Ten minutes later, Lanois ambled into the hotel room, wearing a plaid, flannel shirt under a sleeveless jacket. His long, black hair was thinning slightly in front, and there was about two days' worth of beard stubble on his chin. He was a hotel security manager's nightmare; I had trouble figuring out how different he would look shaved and showered.

Daniel Lanois was riding the edge of a very large wave that winter. His debut solo album, *Acadie*, had been released to critical acclaim; he had produced, in quick succession, Peter Gabriel's album *So*, Bob Dylan's *Oh, Mercy*, and Robbie Robertson's solo comeback album; and CBC Television's *Man Alive* had spent a full program examining his *spirituality*. It was a long way from the jerry-rigged recording studio he and his brother Bob built in their mother's basement in Hamilton in the 1970s.

"It was your typical recreation room," Lanois told me, smiling benignly. "We put egg cartons on the walls and it was a concrete basement with a dead-solid sound. When I hear recordings now that were done there, they're good . . . really deep sounding."

The Lanois brothers were recording musicians like Willie P. Bennett, Ian and Sylvia Tyson, and Joe Hall and the Continental Drift. During one of those sessions with the Drift, Lanois jumped to his feet and demanded that a certain sound be dropped from one of the tracks because he thought it would end up badly. It was an early demonstration of his ear for sound. The band ignored him. Bass player Paul Quarrington — now a highly respected author — admitted to me later that Lanois had been right, the result turned out to be "awful."

"I really loved those guys," Lanois laughed. "I wanted to make sure they did the right thing."

The brothers made enough cash to build a 24-track studio in downtown Hamilton ("Me and Bob, we always knew we would get out of the basement"), and more work started rolling in: everything from rock to country. During this period, Lanois began experimenting with the textures and moods of sound, and one of his tapes made its way to New York City and into the earshot of English musician-producer Brian Eno. Eno called the brothers and booked studio time, and the result was a friendship and creative relationship that Lanois said influenced his work permanently.

"It was an interesting phase of my life," Lanois explained, "a sort of experimental, more atmospheric period. I remember being in the studio for weeks on end, working on these sounds on the console — textures and regeneration — and coming up with the strangest combinations. It was great . . . very musical."

It was the collaboration with Brian Eno that led Lanois to Peter Gabriel. But I was most interested in his relationship with Bob Dylan.

Lanois is renowned for his single-minded conviction that he is always right, and I was intrigued by what sort of chemistry developed when he worked with musical legends, like Dylan, who had strong opinions of their own. "Intimidation is insecurity," was all he said. Then he continued: "When somebody tries to use intimidation as a means to overcome a problem, it's usually a sign that they are insecure in some way. So the best way to deal with that is to supply them with even more confidence, to let them believe that you're there to help them, that you're their friend, and usually clarity and honesty will cut through any of that nonsense."

This technique, which sounded to me like part sycophantic stroking and part self-help program, had provided Lanois with enough resources to maintain the Hamilton studio, open a second one in New Orleans, and buy a home in England. As he toured in support of *Acadie*, he carried with him state-of-the-art DAT recording equipment so he could put together his second album, *For the Beauty of Wynona*, at the same time. "As I write the songs, I think I'll record them this time. Then, when I have enough for a record, that's when it will come out. Most people have access to that technique, especially these days when every corner you turn, there's a tape recorder. I don't think it's such a luxury." He gave me an enigmatic, close-lipped smile. "It's just a matter of timing. Understanding timing is the luxury."

◻

Here's the thing about Tori Amos: everybody who interviews her comes away thinking they've just gotten one of the most frank, revealing, and intimate confessions ever given by someone in the public spotlight. Often they are right. I was no exception to this rule; when I spoke with her in 1992, just after the release of her million-selling, remarkable album *Little Earthquakes*, I felt as if I had gone through an encounter session.

When I met her, I was equipped with the basic facts: she had to go to England to make it in the music business, she was perpetually embarrassed about her brief fling in a bad rock band called Y Kant Tori Read, and the songs on her first solo record were so personal and revealing that, as the *Toronto Star's* Peter Howell put it at the time, they "simultaneously make the listener want to sing along, while reaching for the telephone speed dial button to the suicide prevention hotline." I knew that, armed with just her voice and her piano, she could bring a rowdy, beer-soaked bar to a total standstill.

Tori Amos is a small — *petite* is actually the word that springs to mind, yet it is somehow very inappropriate — and intense woman, with a frizzy halo of red hair, pale skin, and a humorous twinkle in her eye. When we sat down to talk in a private office in her hotel, she pulled her chair in front of mine so that our knees were touching, leaned forward intently while speaking and listening, often laying a hand on my arm or knee to emphasize a point, and locked eyes with me for what I swear was the entire length of the interview.

"Things get really exciting when people are uncomfortable," she said. At that moment I wasn't about to argue. "Because that's when you know you can maybe have an interesting conversation with somebody, instead of, you've rehearsed all your lines all your life on how you want people to view you, so you know just the right answers that you want to give so they can't know too much about you, and *you* can't know too much about you. I get excited when a person alone at the piano can make people really . . . ," she paused, groping for a description. "I want to think of a word here . . . vulnerable . . . nervous . . . hard-core? That's a lot of feeling that comes out of just an acoustic instrument, because in our mind an acoustic instrument is a nice, polite thing and I don't think what I do is about nice. I'm a kind person, sometimes. As far as being confessional, I'm not asking for approval. It's not 'tell me I'm okay,' it's 'I'm gonna talk about what's really going on in this conversation, the subtext that nobody wants to talk about.' We all know how brilliant everybody is, we all know that we're all geniuses, we all know that we've got no problems, so let's talk about what really isn't going on."

When I asked her how she could bring that level of emotion to a performance nearly every night and still maintain her sanity, she laughed. "I'm a wreck. I've been a wreck for awhile because this year we may have already done two hundred shows — when I say *we*, I'm alone up there, so I guess it's just me and all the other girls inside." She stopped again, as if this thought had just occurred to her for the first time.

"It's a constant focusing that I have to do," she continued. "Tonight I'll bring something different to the show than I brought to the show in Philly last week. I'm not foolish enough to think that I can just walk out there and be in the head-space to do this material. There's a different girl that talks to you than the girl that goes out and plays — she never does interviews. I have to prepare myself emotionally to go out there. It's very draining on one level and yet exhilarating at the same time.

"When you run a marathon, you expend a lot of energy, but there are certain places that you reach because there's a freedom. When I reach it, and sometimes it only lasts for seconds, I cannot think of anything else but that moment. The greatest freedom I reach is when I'm not thinking about where I have to be the next day or what I'm going to eat later or what I'm going to say to such-and-such because, you know, we had this big row, whatever it is. I'm in that moment, hitting that note, we're all going God-knows-where together on some other dimension, where time and space doesn't exist anymore. And maybe it only lasts for a second but that moment is like nothing I've ever experienced."

One Sunday afternoon in August of 1991, Tori Amos went to a matinee showing of *Thelma and Louise*, "expecting nothing more than a few hours of respite." During the film, she came face-to-face with memories of her own sexual assault seven years earlier, an assault she had, until then, chosen to forget. The result was the song "Me and a Gun," a graphic and nerve-wracking description of the incident.

"I wrote the song that afternoon, performed it that night, and it's almost as if it has a life of its own," she said quietly. "It comes and gives me a hug and says, 'just let me do what I'm supposed to do and trust that you're going to be okay, but you have to do this.' So, during the next year of singing and talking about it, I didn't realize how much I'd be talking about it, and I didn't real-ize how I was going to have to confront the experience itself. You see, I didn't get help when it happened — I didn't talk about it at all. I didn't acknowledge it. I became this invincible we-will-never-be-hurt-again. So I cut it out.

"Now that I'm looking back, I'm having to deal with seven years," she paused for a beat and swallowed hard, "of how it affected my personal life, seven years of how I've been shameful in my own mind. But at the same time, there is a belief that I have that, no matter what has happened to us, we have a choice on how we want to live our lives from today on. Now, do I live my life as a woman who can't have a healthy sexual relationship because I equate that one experience with sex? And it is not sex, it is violence . . . and it has nothing to do with a relationship between a man that you care about and you, nothing to do with that act. So I've had to be very disciplined and refuse to crawl into that place of victimization, where you can stay for the rest of your life."

❏

In 1988, Mary Margaret O'Hara released her first album, *Miss America*, to rave critical reviews, and I told her she dressed like my mom.

We were sitting on the grass at the Mariposa Festival in June of that year and O'Hara had just finished one of her quirky, spasmodic, lyrical, and very entertaining performances. She was dressed in what appeared to be nothing but double knits and polyester, in colours that honestly reminded me of those long-ago days with my mom working in the kitchen of our suburban home.

"Allll right!!!" she laughed, "I *am* your mom . . . ," then she began singing, "*Talk to meeeee* . . . ," and dissolved into giggles. "What do you mean, like your mom?" All mock seriousness. "At what part of the day? Because, you see, I kept these pants on over a dress. I thought it looked kind of cultish, scared me half to death."

The sister of SCTV's Catherine O'Hara, Mary Margaret had done a bit of acting herself (she and her sister were The Lemon Twins to John Candy and Eugene Levy's Schmenge Brothers in *The Last Polka* in 1984), but was better known as part of a couple of Toronto's Queen Street West bands, Songship and Go Deo Chorus. O'Hara was given a recording contract on her own after a friend sent five of her Go Deo Chorus songs to Virgin Records.

O'Hara is a unique performer. Her lilting, fluid voice dips and careens around, swooping from peaks to valleys and sounding, as one ecstatic reviewer put it, "like a violin." Her physical performance is no less interesting. She continually punches the air with a clenched fist in a curious, arrhythmic fashion, *against* the beat. This action is so contrary to what the ears are hearing, and it is so difficult to do, that it appears to be simultaneously intentional and unconscious.

"Back in Ottawa last year, someone said 'I can't look at her, I can't, she just makes me sick,'" O'Hara told me with astonishment. "It's on my beat! I kind of throw things in, because if you don't feel too loose, you just want to . . . ," she shuddered, "OOOOOHHHHHH . . . jump out of your skin, so you're kind of rocking it up a bit. But there are all these relationships that I set up in music and sometimes I find it odd that people don't hear it more readily."

Many critics, and even some musicians, also had trouble with O'Hara's odd lyrical flights that often seemed out of place when laid atop the musical accompaniment. "It went for a lot of years with them saying, 'I'm not playing that! I'm not going to play that against that!' And you run into trouble at times when you have very good takes on things and then once in awhile things can fall apart.

"It's funny," she was thoughtful, "you set it up very strongly and then, you don't pull it apart, you stay in there, but you improvise around it. So sometimes, if you're not feeling on or somebody moves out of their area — which is fine — it can be great, or it can fall apart." She broke into a smile. "It's kinda like the weather . . . chancy, in a way?" she laughed. "But it's actually all set up. I write like that, where I'll set up odd things but they're very natural to my ear. But only in the years in the past that I've come up against people who've said, 'You can't do that!' So I just kept doing it, because it's so natural to my ear."

Because of that peculiar perspective on arrangements, O'Hara said she has chosen her backup musicians for their abilities to be unconstrained and their capacities to translate her musical ideas into the written form of musical charts. "I'll write the parts like a bass, guitar, and drum thing. The rest of it, on certain songs, is structured to sound like improvising. I have to get people to write it because it's all out of my head . . . so, I'll sit there and they'll go, 'Oh, that's seven-eight . . . wait a minute, sing it again . . . ' It's very strange. I wouldn't want to have to go to school to learn what I know naturally in my head because I'd be so far behind."

Part of the appeal for listeners to O'Hara's music is the ability to get lost in the sounds — the seemingly endless twists and curls of the melody and the lyrics. O'Hara said her nervousness before live audiences prevented her from feeling that way while she was singing. "I can get lost a lot more readily in recording when I finally sing than I can in front of people. You can't count on it live and you've also got all kinds of people in front of you, which makes me feel like, 'What am I doing being looked at? Why aren't they up here?' So I can't really get going."

1.5

The Backlash Kids

A couple of months after I met Jay McInerney, he appeared on the cover of *Esquire* magazine dressed like a ninja, leaping in the air and brandishing a sword. "Jay McInerney skewers his critics," the caption read.

McInerney had plenty of targets. Since the success of his novel *Bright Lights, Big City,* and his consistent appearances in gossip columns and tabloids, he had been under heavy attack for both his writing style and his lifestyle. He and his contemporaries, Bret Easton Ellis and Tama Janowitz, had become known as the Literary Brat Pack — a reference to the thespian Brat Pack of young upstart actors a few years earlier.

I never met Ellis, but interviewed Janowitz — twice — and McInerney. Liked her, hated him springs to mind here, but while I wasn't impressed with McInerney's supercilious defensiveness, I can't say he was anything other than the product of the events that had happened to him at that time.

During the mid- to late eighties, this triumvirate was considered the cutting edge of American fiction, much as Canadian writer Douglas Coupland would be touted in the early nineties.

McInerney's first novel was called *Ransom,* and Janowitz had begun with one called *American Dad,* both in the early part of the decade. But it was his *Bright Lights, Big City* in 1984 and her *Slaves of New York* at around the same time that really established their presence. In 1985, Bret Easton Ellis wrote *Less Than Zero*. The troika was complete and the critical barrage began.

McInerney maintained that anyone who mistook a sentence from *Bright Lights, Big City* with a sentence from *Less Than Zero* should go back to Prose 101. He was right. *Bright Lights, Big City* told of a young, separated magazine fact-checker, caught up in the New York City whirl of cocaine and clubs. *Less Than Zero* gave a dispassionate accounting of the numbed lives of rich, aimless Hollywood movie brats. McInerney's novel did a creditable job of developing characters; *Less Than Zero* had the feel of having been written by a machine — shallow and emotionless. The Janowitz book, *Slaves of New York*, was a pastiche of that city's art scene in the eighties, done up as short stories. The only things that each had in common were the presence of the 1980s drug of choice, cocaine, and the fact that each was turned into a mediocre movie.

The film version of *Bright Lights, Big City* came closest to success with Michael J. Fox in the lead. *Less Than Zero* in the hands of Hollywood was turned from an unflinching, if pointless, slice of youthful decadence into a true-friends, true-love morality tale. The movie plot bore virtually no resemblance to the story line of the novel.

Slaves of New York had a better film pedigree but a worse box-office fate. Andy Warhol had optioned several of the stories in the collection and, after Janowitz's subsequent novel, *A Cannibal in Manhattan*, was published, he asked her to write the screenplay. When Warhol died, the prestigious film duo of Merchant and Ivory bought the rights and Janowitz rewrote her material in collaboration with James Ivory.

It was an experience she said she enjoyed completely, because Merchant and Ivory had collaborated with writer Ruth Jhabvala for thirty years, and were used to working with a woman. Janowitz praised the final result, which starred Bernadette Peters, as funny, interesting, and true to the New York art scene of the time. But movie audiences were underwhelmed and the film sprinted straight to video.

"It got very bad reviews very quickly," Janowitz told me, "which I think was rather unfair. I think they just gang up on something and decide, we don't like this. But, in fact, people who have been renting it on video have said to me how much they enjoyed it. Maybe at some future time it will be re-evaluated."

It was not unsubstantiated paranoia that made Janowitz, Ellis, and McInerney feel critics were ganging up on them and their work. As McInerney noted in his *Esquire* article, "Janowitz hasn't done herself any favors by doing ads. Selling your credibility to the highest corporate bidder does compromise your contract with readers insofar as you wish to speak to them about matters of life and death." That being said, McInerney went on to defend Janowitz's position as the efforts of the artist to pay the rent. Everybody is implicated, McInerney contended, and he advised the cultural gatekeepers to take two Tylenols and relax; the walls, he said, will still be standing in the morning.

But while Janowitz was being slammed for crass commercialism, McInerney was being pilloried for his love of New York nightlife. The clear implication was that if he could be a shallow publicity pig, how serious and how good could his writing be?

Well, pretty damn good, as it turns out. *Bright Lights, Big City* is a good book. Unlike *Less Than Zero*, it is genuinely funny and well written. By itself it established McInerney's place in contemporary American fiction. But the accompanying fame and attention, if not fortune, had little to do with any of that. Tabloids, gossip columns, and, especially, the stinging satire of *Spy* magazine, under the editorship of Canadian E. Graydon Carter, chronicled McInerney's seemingly endless nights of clubs, booze, women, and maybe even the drugs he wrote about.

"Yeah, it does bother me sometimes," McInerney said when I asked him about it. "On the one hand, it just sort of goes with the territory and I'd be lying if I said a little bit of it isn't fun. But, on the other hand, I do get a little annoyed when I wake up in the morning and go out and buy the papers and find out what I was supposedly doing the night before. And I say 'supposedly' because very often it isn't true."

When I met him, McInerney was the very picture of the young, literate New England writer. Clean-shaven and darkly all-American looking, he was actually wearing a tweed jacket over a turtleneck sweater. All that was missing was the pipe and the leather elbow patches. But this image of the retiring bookworm quickly evaporated once the writer got into the bar where he was to read from his new book. During the course of the evening, he managed to get the telephone number of every blonde woman in the room. Then, while being driven to the airport, he blithely tore the numbers into shreds and tossed them out the car window.

To me, he grandly insisted that front-row-centre life experience is essential if the writer is to accurately reflect society. But living this philosophy, he claimed, had its downside.

"At this point I'm concerned that I not attract more attention than my work. Edmund Wilson, one of our greatest literary critics, once said of *The Great Gatsby* — arguably the greatest American novel — that it was a book about the drinking habits of rich Long Islanders. Well, as a matter of fact, it *is* about the drinking habits of rich Long Islanders, but it's also a great American novel.

"I think that for a writer like myself, it's your job to reflect — to hold a mirror up to — the society you live in, even if the society doesn't always like what it sees when it looks into that mirror. You know, there's a difference between writing about a decadent culture and decadent writing."

Yet McInerney's behaviour seemed uncomfortably close to his own words from *Bright Lights, Big City*. "You were gathering experience for a novel," he wrote. "You went to parties with writers, cultivated a writerly persona. You wanted to be Dylan Thomas without the paunch, F. Scott Fitzgerald without the crack-up. You wanted to skip over the dull grind of actual creation."

That dull grind of actual creation seemed to have been avoided in McInerney's follow-up novel, *Story of My Life*, which looked like a pale attempt to justify his own taste for the party life by writing a book about it. Worse, he had tried to cover it with a sheen of art by writing from the point of view of a young woman. The book was promoted heavily. It came with tank tops emblazoned with the book title on the front and a large razor blade chopping lines of cocaine on the back. Nobody was buying — not even his readers.

But even with this failure, and putting aside his personal habits, there is little question that Jay McInerney is a writer of talent.

For that matter, so is Tama Janowitz, though to a lesser degree. Her follow-up novel, *A Cannibal in Manhattan*, suffered the same fate as *Story of My Life*. Yet she said to stop writing was out of the question simply because it was a vocation over which she had no control. "Oh, I hate writing so much," she moaned. "It's just agony to me. I don't have a choice about it, but I don't like doing it. The only time for me that it is a joy is when I forget about me and become the character."

In McInerney's case, the intervention of a respected and accomplished writer may have saved both him and his writing talent from a life of pop-star superficiality. The late poet and author Raymond Carver had given high praise to *Bright Lights, Big City* when it was published, calling it "a rambunctious, deadly funny novel."

At the time, McInerney was, perhaps not surprisingly, enamoured with writers who had pushed themselves to extremes, believing that abuse and suffering were necessary primers for a solid life of creativity.

"There's this myth about the inspired, lunatic artist," he said. "If you read about Hemingway or Fitzgerald, you'd think, if only I drink enough I'll be a really good writer. But Carver himself was a reformed alcoholic and it was nice to see somebody living a stable and not necessarily self-destructive life."

In the mid-eighties, Ray Carver was teaching at Syracuse University in upper New York State. He and McInerney had met, become friends, and begun a correspondence. Perhaps Carver realized the temptations and pitfalls facing a successful new author, or perhaps it was just that he recognized a talent in need of protection and encouragement. Whatever his reasons, Carver encouraged McInerney to leave New York City. He arranged a fellowship to study English literature and urged the young novelist to practise his craft by writing every day.

For his part, while it was at its peak, the brouhaha of tabloid gossip surrounding them was not especially distasteful to McInerney.

"It has its drawbacks," he told me. "It's very hard to lead a private life when your every move is being reported in the gossip columns. And it's not something I expected as a writer. If I'd decided to be an actor, if I were Tom Cruise, this is what you would hope for, and it wasn't at all what I had hoped for as a writer.

"On the other hand, I'm having a lot of fun doing it and I have the time to write full time now — I don't have to hold down a second job, I don't have to teach, I don't have to bartend, which is one of the things I was doing. And an awful lot of people are reading my books, so I feel really lucky."

Tama Janowitz reacted to the backlash with resigned humour. "They never seemed to realize that I never got the first part," she laughed with just the slightest trace of bitterness. "You know, the part where you're praised too much? I didn't get the praise part. They just jumped to the conclusion that, she's gotten a lot of attention, it must have been good publicity, we're going to teach her a lesson and say how bad this is. So I got the bad part. Now I'm hoping I'll get the good part."

After the tepid response to their newer work, both Janowitz and McInerney withdrew from the scene for several years while their contemporary, Bret Easton Ellis, continued to publish amid alternating groans (for the tedious *The Rules of Attraction*) and cries of outrage (the execrable *American Psycho*). Each reappeared in 1992 with a new novel. Janowitz's *The Male Cross-Dresser Support Group* sank without a ripple. McInerney's *Brightness Falls* garnered serious praise. The backlash had died away and others had assumed the mantle of Bright, Young Things Deserving To Be Crushed.

By the spring of 1994 Janowitz was back paying the rent by appearing in magazine computer ads and was likely wondering what ever happened to the good part. The answer wasn't hard to find: for at least three years, it had been unrelentingly lavished on the young writer from British Columbia named Douglas Coupland.

By 1994 Coupland had written three books: *Generation X*, the title of which the insatiable media phrasemakers of pop culture had commandeered for their own; *Shampoo Planet*; and a collection of short stories called *Life After God*.

Life After God was Coupland's swan dive into pretension. If it had been his first attempt at writing it might have been forgivable, but certainly not publishable. It was sophomoric and affected, "infused," as reviewer Bruce Handy put it in *Vanity Fair* magazine, "with the hothouse nostalgia and premature weariness of high school seniors harking back to the Eden of junior year."

Just so. Yet the tide of admiration for Coupland seemed to have reached the stage at which the product of his "dull grind of actual creation" seemed beside the point. He had become a nineties postmodern phenomenon and it was practically incidental whether he wrote anything at all.

A few months before Conrad Black crowbarred him out of the editor's job at *Saturday Night* magazine, the rapidly aging John Fraser featured an excerpt from *Life After God* and opened the magazine with his own story about Coupland. I was left gasping for air as Fraser, in an unseemly attempt to document that he had known Coupland, you know, like, before *Generation X*, called him "brilliant," "a new-minted McLuhan," "Homer to the microserfs," and "the Jack Kerouac of his generation."

Hold on, I thought. Character, plot, dramatic tension, comedy, a pleasing or creative new use of the language, descriptive words and phrases — were these not the hallmarks of good writing? *Generation X* had been a clever, if uneven, book that presented some amusing (though oddly written without a hint of humour) reference points for the jobless generation in its twenties. But its unfocused style and McNuggets of ideas left an unsatisfying sense of incompletion for the reader.

Shampoo Planet cranked the age demographic down a notch further, presenting the dilemmas of postmodern life as faced by a clutch of kids in their late teens. A week after I had read it, I couldn't remember a thing about it. Was that good literature? Were future generations going to recall Tyler — I think his name was Tyler — hanging around the empty mall in *Shampoo Planet* the way another generation remembered Holden Caulfield checking into that hotel or Sal and Dean rolling into San Francisco?

It also occurred to me that the age gap between the thirty-something Coupland and his subjects in *Shampoo Planet* was the same as that between him and me. I couldn't help but imagine the shrieks of outrage if someone of my generation dared to write an entire book claiming to capture the voice of those in their thirties. Yet Coupland had seemed to convince nearly everybody that he knew what was happening — apparently not much — in the minds of the younger set.

In *Life After God*, which came with its own audiotape version read by the author, Coupland lived up to at least one of John Fraser's assessments: he was "brave, very brave" to have tried his hand at introspection. The clever McNuggets of *Generation X* had been abandoned for a set of sickly sweet, hollow-centred vacuities, to wit: "My body grows old, it turns strange colors, refuses orders, becomes less and less a part of the me I remember

I once was. I read what I have written here and realize that I am not a happy person and maybe I never will be." Not a "new-minted McLuhan" so much as a recycled Rod McKuen, duking it out with Robert James Waller to see who could bang the gong of banality more often.

I met Douglas Coupland briefly at a booksellers' convention in Toronto in the wake of the tremendous success of *Generation X*. Tall, pale, and distracted, he appeared to be uncomfortable in that milieu. A few months later I was sent an advance copy of *Shampoo Planet*, in anticipation of an interview.

While I was unimpressed with the book, I was mindful of what had happened to McInerney, Janowitz, et al., and also that second books rarely live up to expectations. I was, in other words, ready to cut him some slack.

I can think of no other way to represent what transpired at our meeting fairly, other than to provide a straight verbatim transcript of parts of the conversation. When Doug Coupland walked into my studio — twenty minutes late for the booking — I was prepared to like him. By the time he left, I thought he was a spoiled, insufferable, egotistical little snot, lacking in grace, courtesy, generosity, and ideas.

Before we began, he told me he had had only two or three hours sleep and was not feeling himself. I would have taken this seriously if I hadn't heard him give the same excuse a week or so earlier to Peter Gzowski on "Morningside." He said he wanted me to only ask him "specific" questions, nothing general — he didn't want to have to perform any mental gymnastics. As we sat down in the studio, he asked me my name. He then wrote K-E-N in large letters on a scrap of paper and propped it in front of him. Not, I remember thinking, an auspicious beginning.

I was aware that Coupland had had trouble selling *Generation X* and that he had been rejected by a large number of publishers, many of them Canadian, before St. Martin's Press in New York published him. I found that an interesting fact and I told him, just before the tape rolled, that I would begin the interview by asking about it.

"You spent a lot of time flogging *Generation X* around to different publishers and not having much success for the longest time, right?"

"Wait, wait, wait . . . [looking down at the scrap of paper] . . . Ken . . . that's a horrible way to start this. That's unnecessary, using the word 'flog.' It's pejorative and it's not the way it happened."

Deep breath. "You tried to sell this book to publishers for how long, before somebody picked it up?"

"Well, my agent, bless him he's dead now, he had tried selling it around Canada first and then in the States but, you know, back then I don't think it's not selling in Canada first was any sort of function of Canada. I think that's just the nature of the work. I mean, two years or three years ago there was no general consensus that there was any form of any younger sensibility other than The Baby Boomer, which was this monolith that went from everyone from Jane Fonda down to, you know . . . aahhh . . . you know, Rick Schroder or something. It was just crazy. You know. And uh . . . for instance . . . [looking down] . . . Ken . . . if we'd been having this same discussion one year ago in 1991, instead of 1992, you'd probably be saying, you know, 'what makes you think there's even some sort of generation?' When I was doing what little bit of radio I did last year, I was having to defend the whole notion of something different. I don't get that anymore."

"Defend it in what sense? You mean that there was a real antagonism to it?"

"No, that it even exists, you know. So I think that's how much general sensibilities have changed in the last year even. And even the year before that it was, like, 'what's this guy going on about? Is he on drugs?' So that's, you know, why it was hard to sell at the beginning and in the end we found a wonderful editor down in New York who is an off-beat guy. And he was like, yeah, well, cool, whatever, let's try it."

"At the time you were going around making those defences would have been about the same time you were writing the next one, *Shampoo Planet*, where you are dealing with a whole other generation —"

"Yeah, well, I write. That's what I do, so I'm going to do it regardless and, aaahhhh . . . uhmmmm [ten-second pause] . . . you lost me, sorry . . ."

"Was it disconcerting to be in the situation where you are going around doing interviews defending one thing — the *Generation X* book and what you represented in it — at the same time you're back at home working on *Shampoo Planet* where you're dealing with a younger generation?"

"Oh gosh. Well, I write about characters, not about generations, you know. And I think its the media that puts this whole generation spin on them. Ahhmmmm . . . [fifteen-second pause]"

"Really?" I was gently prodding.

"Ahhhh [looking down] . . . Ken . . . Ken . . . wait, wait . . . Ken, Ken, Ken . . . wait . . . you're being, like, no offence, but kind of like antagonistic here, making it look like what I do is some cynical abusive gesture of my audience, or something . . ."

"No, not at all —"

". . . I mean, I just write what I write and, you know, I don't think about it all that much. I don't plot it or plan it, or anything. And everyone always talks as if I'm like Decima Research or something . . ."

"But that's the situation you found yourself in ultimately, wasn't it? You say you were having to defend *Generation X* —"

"Well, in the end, I just stopped doing interviews because I was tired of it . . . and then the new music scene happened and suddenly I didn't have to prove anything. The same people that were being, you know, sort of, you know, attacking before, were suddenly phoning up and saying 'Oh please, please, please,' you know. So I guess it's just a general shift in perception."

"Tell me about the characters in *Shampoo Planet*. You've taken a character who makes a brief appearance in *Generation X* and put him in a different set of circumstances —"

"That's how the book started out, that seed character, the younger brother Tyler from *Generation X* . . . aaahhhmmm . . . [ten-second pause] . . ."

"A character that was interesting to you when you wrote about him as a subsidiary character in *Generation X*?"

"Uhmmmm . . . [long pause] . . . Hhmmmmm [big sigh] . . ."

"What was it about this guy that was interesting that you wanted to expand on him later on?"

"Yeah, uhmmm . . . well, the whole . . . [long pause] . . . sorry, Ken . . ."

"That's okay."

". . . Ahhh . . . [twenty-second pause] . . . you can edit this out later . . . Oh, I liked . . . I liked his optimism and it's not a forced optimism or an ironic optimism pushed to such an extreme that it appears real. I mean I think it is genuine. You know, I've said before that sometimes we meet people who wish they could live in another century, like, 'oh gee, I wish I could live in the France of Louis XIV, or I wish I could live in Bloomsbury England.' And I think, in a way, I feel like someone who's living in the year 2525, who wished really, really hard that they could live in late twentieth century North America and then I got my wish and so here I am. Oh my god, it's the telephone . . . it's Federal Express . . . it's Burger King . . . wow, how fantastic! I've read about all this in history books and here it is! There's that side of my personality that I think I wanted to get out in a character and that was Tyler.

"You know, I'm always so surprised when people think that I, sort of, don't think that history is important or that I don't think that the future is a great place. I think, boy, we're so lucky to be here now with all these wonderful things and we're always riding ourselves so hard. I mean, we have a fantastic culture, some of the best things ever gotten, ever, in the history of the world and yet we think, like Chicken Little, we think the sky is falling down because we watch a few, you know, weird things on TV all the time over and over. Things are great now. I really think that."

In the rest of this strained and unfocused conversation, Coupland sighed, puffed, and paused his way through his assessment of the crisis facing young people and the joys of our technological society, which has given us "CNN and MTV and fax machines and cellular telephones and affordable PCs and inventory spreadsheets and satellite communications and cable television and the VCR revolution and optical fibre and you name it." The only time he seemed to brighten was when talking about the success of *Generation X*.

"I think they had a heart attack in New York when I handed it in," he said, referring to his New York publishers. "But to their credit they went ahead and did it. I think they had no hopes for it, and I certainly had no hopes for it. I always thought it would just be a charity purchase for a few people I went to high school with. I'm still genuinely amazed that as many people feel the same way about the world, or see it the same way as I do. Because, at the time, I felt like I was all alone in the universe and I feel less so now.

"Another thing is that people think that writers have some secret club they go to where they have cocktails and discuss whether they sharpen pencils. It's the most non-community community going — I think I've met two other fiction writers and they live far away. It's an absolutely solitary activity. And here I am, Mr. I-Don't-Like-Jobs, but I've had a few jobs in my life and I've always enjoyed them, and they were always lots and lots of fun, but I would kind of like to have some kind of job right now. Just for that sense of community, gossiping around the coffee machine, and all the small stuff that goes in offices. I miss that."

John Fraser ended his adulatory piece on Douglas Coupland suggesting he might put a plaque under his desk, where Coupland had huddled after an "abrasive" CBC interview, marking it as a welcome rest stop for other writers to ponder their lives before going on to do "even greater things." Fraser, and probably his desk as well, are no longer at *Saturday Night*. Among those writers who still have pride in their creative skills and who still believe that literature must triumph over marketing and not the reverse, the desire to send out a search party for the desk is about as likely as Douglas Coupland developing a sense of humour.

A Final Word

"Medium Rare" came to an end in the spring of 1993, just two months after the Canadian Radio, Television and Telecommunications Commission removed the requirement for FM radio stations in Canada to have spoken word programming.

I interviewed Douglas Coupland the previous fall, and between that dreary experience and the end of the program I had an opportunity to talk to plenty of other talented people who lifted my spirits and gave me hope about the state of the arts in Canada. In those few months I spoke with very gifted writers like Guy Vanderhaeghe, David Adams Richards, and Matt Cohen; I was entertained by Dennis Lee and Jack Webster; I was impressed by Jane Urquhart and Douglas Glover; and I was awed by John Ralston Saul and bemused by W. P. Kinsella.

I have left radio to tackle the rigours (and believe me, they *are* rigours) of profiling creative people on television. TV is certainly far more challenging and, these days, far more influential than radio. But TV can never equal the sense of intimacy, the feeling of eavesdropping, or the spontaneity and natural flow of an interview on radio that has a beginning, a middle, and an end.

I was reminded of radio's advantages recently when I sat, with a handful of friends, in a late-night bar trading shots of Calvados with the great Russian poet Yevgeny Yevtushenko. As he grandly dominated the table with stories about such wildly diverse people as Boris Yelstin, Warren Beatty, Jerzy Kosinski, and Dick Cavett, I realized that television could never capture a scene like this; only the unobtrusiveness of radio could make listeners feel like they were part of that gathering. I miss it.

I like to believe that maybe someday private radio will return to its glory days. In the meantime, I'm going to still be out there reading books.